WRITING BOOKS FOR CHILDREN

By

Jane Yolen

p.19 publishers' catalogs

Publishers THE WRITER, INC. *Boston*

New Edition
Completely Revised and Enlarged

Library of Congress Cataloging in Publication Data

Yolen, Jane.
    Writing books for children.

    Includes index.
    1. Children's literature—Authorship. I. Title.
PN147.5.Y6 1982   808.06'8   82-13673
ISBN 0-87116-133-8 (pbk.)

Contents

*Books should be tried by a judge
and jury as though they were crimes . . .*
—Samuel Butler

Author's Note

In the world of literature, books for children are usually labeled "juveniles." Children's book writers and illustrators are often approached tentatively by well-meaning friends and relatives who ask—with the kindest of motives—"When are you going to grow up and write a *real* book?" That means, of course, when are you planning to write an adult book. No one would ever ask a pediatrician when he or she was going to grow up and look at adult throats. *That* would be an insult. It is considered a compliment, however, to imply that writers of children's books might be capable of improving and moving up the line to grown-up books. My automatic response to that gentle jab is: "I'd rather write juvenile literature than senile literature."

But that is really begging the question. I don't write specifically for children, or even with a specific child in mind, though that is a time-honored way of beginning a book ever since the Reverend Charles Dodgson took the Liddell sisters for a boat ride on the Thames and told them the story that became *Alice in Wonderland.* I simply write a story. I begin it at the beginning and finish it at its natural end. Sometimes what I have written is a story for small children; sometimes for what is, peculiarly enough, called the middle-aged child; and sometimes for that rare beast known in library circles as the Young Adult. The designation of readership is after the fact. Indeed, that is the editor's prerogative—placing age limits on a book. I have always, myself, subscribed to Arthur Ransome's philosophy of writing for children: "You write not for children but for yourself. And if by good fortune children enjoy what you enjoy, why then you are a writer of children's books . . . no special credit to you, but simply thumping good luck!"

However, I suspect that the real reason that what I write most often turns out to be for children is that from an early age I immersed myself in children's books and literature. As a child I read folk and fairy tales, fantasy stories, Nancy Drew mysteries, horse books, and anything by Rudyard Kipling, Robert Louis Stevenson, and Walter Terhune. I read many of these stories still. Some of them have stood the test of the ages—mine as well as theirs. Others have been replaced by newer selections.

Children still read Nancy Drew as well as the latest of the young adult fads—like teen romances—in the tens of thousands. In addition to *The Secret Garden,* that perennial favorite of Frances Hodgson Burnett's titles, elementary school boys and girls read as many of Judy Blume's novels as they can get their hands on: *Are You There, God? It's Me Margaret, Superfudge, Blubber,* and others. Family books like *Little Women* sit side by side on the shelves with books about broken homes and broken lives: *The Great Gilly Hopkins,* by Katherine Paterson (about a foster child); *Steffie Can't Come Out to Play,* by Fran Arrick (about teen-age prostitution); *The Lottery Rose,* by Irene

Hunt (about child abuse)—all popular with and widely read by pre-teens and young adults.

And so I come to what I consider the only unbreakable rule in writing for children: *If you want to be a writer of books for children, you must be a reader of children's books.* Read all the *good* books you missed as a child. Re-read all the books you considered great as a child. Go to the library and cultivate the children's librarian. Browse in bookstores. Read to your children or to other people's children. Read the award-winning books and the runners-up (often the better stories). As you read, you will unconsciously begin to form your own opinion about children's books. That is what will lead you into writing good books for children.

That is what this book is about—writing *good* books for children. There is too much in the field that is simply no good at all. Of the more than two thousand new children's books published yearly, probably fewer than a hundred are really worthwhile, long lasting, meaty literature. The rest are *litter*-ature. Don't add to the larger list, for our children deserve the best.

Maia Wojciechowska, a Newbery Award winner, declared at a writers conference, "I'm not going to let you inflict your incompetence on defenseless children." I would not make such a statement. Children are stronger than Ms. Wojciechowska thinks, and they will weed out the really bad books. They have kept *Robinson Crusoe, Gulliver's Travels,* and *Mary Poppins* alive, despite the attempts of censors, educators, and Walt Disney to relegate these books to the historical trash bin. Your "incompetence" will more likely be visited upon the hapless parents, grandparents, and maiden aunts who purchase books and often mistake sentimentality (Joan Walsh Anglund's *A Friend Is Someone Who Likes You*) or oversimplification (Richard Bach's

Jonathan Livingston Seagull) or cheapness (the 79-cent supermarket storybook) or full-color reproduction (many of the European imports) for good children's literature.

The object of this book, then, is threefold: First, to show you the broader view of children's books. What was once a fireside tale is now big business. Second, to show you the wide range of children's literature, which extends from the adapted fairy and folk tales to realistic books about drugs, divorce, and death. And, finally, to show you the many opportunities open to anyone who wants to try WRITING BOOKS FOR CHILDREN.

—Jane Yolen
Phoenix Farm

1

Down the Rabbit Hole— and Why

THERE IS a story that is told about Stanislavsky, the great theater director. One day a well-known actor came to see him.

"Counsel me," the actor begged. "Tell me what to do. I have always performed for adults. Tomorrow I must do a play in front of an audience of children."

Stanislavsky never hesitated. "Act as you always do," he replied. "Only better!"

So, too, when you write for children, you must write as you always do. Only better.

In an adult book you might gloss over events or let your diction get a bit wobbly. You might change a character's hair color or turn the heroine's eyes from green to blue halfway through the book. The average adult reader will forgive you. Not the child.

It is the adult—reader and writer—who often does not realize how important a book is to a child. The child never underestimates its importance.

Real writing

Would-be writers of juvenile books are taken in by the kind of thinking that goes into the misleading: "Learn to write. Start with children's books." Courses in children's literature are usually nicknamed "Kiddy Lit," which is both cute and condescending.

When a well-known editor of adult books read one of my books she looked up with genuine surprise and said: "But that is *real* writing. It doesn't sound like a children's book at all." She meant it as a compliment.

Real writing! Did she mean real vs. false? Real vs. plastic? Real vs. made? Real vs. unreal? I know what she meant. She meant that it was not overly sweet, simplistic, and flat-footed in its prose.

What the editor or the kiddy lit students or the would-be writers of juveniles refuse to see is that, in Eleanor Cameron's words, children's literature "does not exist in a world of its own, but is enmeshed in a larger world of literature."

Literature and books. It is important to see that there is a distinction between them. It is a distinction that any adult will make when talking about writing for adults. Yet these same adults find it impossible to see the difference when considering writing for children. All reading for young people is lumped together.

But children's literature is as great as any literature for adults. And children's books are no better and no worse than adult books—except for one very important aspect. Children's books, whether literature or no, change lives.

Writing in *The New York Times* not so long ago, editor-critic John Leonard said: "Books, if they are any good, and even if they are significantly bad, have consequences. They are part of our cultural respiration . . . they alter attitudes and perceptions . . . [they] change lives."

He was talking about adult books. I think he would have been closer to the mark had he been talking about books for young readers. Adult books *maintain* lives more than change lives. And empty books maintain empty lives.

As adults, we are used to the inaccuracies, distortions, half-truths, and whole lies served up in print. We read cynically, with a kind of built-in despair we sometimes disguise as sentimentality. We look for rainbows, knowing that the pot of gold is full of rainwater at best.

We are already changed, you see.

Species gap

Do you remember in *Mary Poppins* when the Banks twins are listening to the starling and are told that, like it or not, they will forget how to talk to the animals as they grow up? It is the price of becoming an adult. They don't believe it, of course. Which of us really believes in the inevitability of change when it applies to ourselves? Yet slowly the Banks twins do forget.

Look at us now. We are grown up. We have forgotten how to talk to the animals, forgotten so much that we do not believe we ever could. And we forget, too, that underneath man is a kind of animal. And so we have forgotten how to talk with one another. Especially to our children. It is not a generation gap. It is a species gap.

For the truth of the matter is that children read with their whole hearts. They may ask at the beginning, "Is it true?" Yet even if you say, "No, it is just a story," it is never *just* a story to them. It is a life to live, an entire and very real life to live. When Coleridge wrote about the "willing suspension of disbelief," he was, without knowing it, defining the way children live every day.

That is what imagination is all about—the willing suspension of disbelief. And if we adults could suspend our disbelief that we could communicate with the birds, we would be talking with every passing starling. But we cannot (perhaps we dare not) suspend our disbelief. It would make us childish in our own eyes. Our approach to imagination becomes pedestrian in our later years. We need intermediaries. This intermediary approach was best characterized by an advertisement I saw recently. It was an ad for Florida's Disney World. It read: *To reach the Magic Kingdom, call your travel agent.*

Approaches and attitudes

There are essentially three ways of writing for children. They are also three ways of living, in case you care to apply them. But know this: in the words of science fiction writer Harlan Ellison, "You are what you write." And conversely, you write what you are.

The three ways of writing are these: 1. benign indifference; 2. creative outrage; and 3. take joy.

Benign indifference means that as a writer you are indifferent to your subject, uninvolved with your characters, even at times unenthusiastic about the project on which you are working. It is a term that too often describes the hack writer. It is what can happen if you write for a living instead of living for your writing.

All writing, like life, should be approached with passion, whether passion for a subject, character, or twist of plot. You must be *involved,* or you do not involve your reader. This is especially true when you are writing for children. The reason?

It lies in this passage from C. S. Lewis' *An Experiment in Criticism*: ". . . the first reading of some literary work is often . . . an experience so momentous, that only experiences of love, religion, or bereavement can furnish a standard of comparison."

If you write with benign indifference, you might as well be setting down a term paper for which you need a C in order to pass, or a grocery list, or a thank-you for the thirteenth casserole dish you have received as a wedding present. And you should expect your readers to be just as indifferent to what you have set down.

That kind of writing might be called *ho-humming* a book. Being unresponsive to the needs of your characters or manipulating them to suit the plot rather than letting them grow organically are typical symptoms of an author suffering from benign indifference.

It is easier, of course, to be indifferent. But no one has ever said writing is easy. Writing is one of the hardest ways I know to make a living. It is also one of the hardest ways I know to make life. Oh, you can make surrogate life with relative ease—using benign indifference. But to make a book that will really live, you need passion.

The second way of writing for children is *creative outrage*. When an author wants to imprint on the minds of his young readers certain facts or attitudes, he writes in this manner. But what usually happens is that the result is either a moralistic or a didactic book.

The earliest books for young readers were just this kind. Published in 1563, John Foxe's *Actes and Monuments of These Latter Perilous Days,* known as *The Book of Martyrs,* became the Puritan child's bedside companion. The young readers were instructed to emulate the religious martyrs who went piously through life and joyously to death, and much detail was spent on each maiming, each brutality. The message of the medium was quite clear. The threat of Hell hung quite heavily over the young readers' heads.

By the nineteenth century, a new threat hung over the reader's head—the threat of Information. The Creative Outragers had struck again. The followers of Rousseau—all ladies with three names I call Didactresses—brought this kind of writing for youngsters to full flower. They insisted on giving children the full measure of their own narrow learning. Each story, each tale, was not to amuse but to teach.

Didacticism and moralism are with us again today. Librarians crying out for more and more factual books have helped bring about this renaissance of didacticism. We are in a technological period, and too often the idea is to cram a child from age one with assorted figures and facts, to prepare him for life.

But there is a difference between a good, solid nonfiction book and a didactic one. (See chapter 6 for more on this subject.)

Moralism, too, is flowering again. Only as practitioners of the newest art of public relations, we don't call it that. We call it The New Realism. In books of The New Realism, adult writers try to teach young readers all they should know about the dangers of drugs, drink, divorce, and other assorted sordid realities.

Both the didactic books and the moralistic books are written with "creative outrage." At its worst, this kind of writing is tract writing, propagandizing.

I call it creative outrage instead of just rage because the prefix *out* continues the thrust of the anger. Rage is something burning only within an individual. Outrage reaches beyond the initial anger and turns the rage into creative action. Books such as *The Pigman* (Paul Zindel) and Newbery winner *Sounder* (William H. Armstrong) are examples of *good* creative outrage. They may not necessarily sound angry, as a revolutionary speech to a mob sounds angry. However, they are defining their anger in literary terms, in extended allegories. They are a working-out of the author's rage against injustice.

The problem with this approach to writing, especially when writing books for children, is the trap of excess teaching and excess moralizing. For example, in our attempts to save the world ecologically, we are sucked into writing a *John and Jane Make a Landfill Dump* or a *Let's Build a Compost Heap* kind of book. We are pointing our literary fingers and feeling virtuous.

Yet when an author does this kind of writing, he has forgotten the first axiom of writing books, and especially writing books for children.

ALWAYS REMEMBER, YOU ARE A STORYTELLER. Not a preacher. Not a prophet. Not hell-bent to save the world through pictures and text. After all, one need not moralize to set a moral. For of course there will be a moral in what you write. You are what you write. You write what you are. (Or as Immanuel Kant says: "We see things not as they are, but as we are.") If you are someone who has real morals and moral value in your life, they will come out all unbidden in your writing.

In C. S. Lewis' words, which I never weary of quoting: "The moral inherent in your books will rise from whatever spiritual roots you have succeeded in striking in the course of your life."

The celebration of life

The third way of writing for children is encompassed in that curious phrase *Take Joy*. It is my favorite. It is the way I write, so it is necessarily the one I commend to you.

The phrase itself comes from a beautiful letter written by

the medieval monk Fra Giovanni. The portion of the letter
that concerns us goes like this: "The gloom of the world is
but a shadow; behind it, yet within our reach, is joy. Take
Joy."

No, I am not a Pollyanna. But I can tell you that as a poet
in college, my world reflected my poetry (and not, curiously,
the other way around). I was plunged by my own writing into
cynicism and despair. Yet today, writing books for children,
I am filled with hope, with joy, with life. Like the Greek toast,
yasu, which means "to life, to joy," I find life and joy inex-
tricably linked. And fine writing, which is a celebration of life,
is therefore—in the deeper sense—joy filled.

This does not mean that there should be no sadness in books
for children, no tears, only happy endings. Sometimes my own
stories are dark, and the happy endings quite mixed with grief.
In *Greyling,* the selchie returns to the sea, leaving his adopted
parents behind on the shore. Danina, in *The Girl Who Loved
the Wind,* chooses to sail away from the enclosed mansion of
her father's heart. Yet behind each sadness there is hope,
there is a chance. Greyling returns once a year to visit his
insular parents and share with them the beauties of the wide,
wide sea. Danina is sailing not only *away from* but *toward,*
away from her father but toward the ever-changing and ever-
challenging real world.

The prophetess Cassandra told what was true, foretold what
was going to happen. Her art was born in sorrow. But storytellers tell what *could* be true, what *is* true in another sense,
and so their art is conceived in joy. The storyteller, especially
the teller of tales for young people, must seek out behind the
shadows and Take Joy.

Once you have looked behind the shadows, you will come
upon the real reason that you are writing for children, writing
good books, writing literature. Ordinary books are opaque and

do not admit or admit of light. But literature is many-faceted, prismatic. Light shines through the excellent books or dances off. And the rainbows it gives shine on and on in a child's life in a thousand different ways.

I am so much smarter, know so much more about everything when I am writing than when I am not.

—Kate Wilhelm

2

Portrait of the Artist as a Young Scrap Heap

YOUR MIND is a scrap heap.

Not a very flattering description perhaps, but an accurate one. Everything you have ever seen, heard, read, felt is stored away in bits and pieces there. Some scraps close to the front are very accessible: phone numbers of friends, the grocery list, the birthdays of your children, your father's favorite shaving lotion, the words of a special song.

Other scraps are shoved so far back, you believe them lost forever. But they are not. They are waiting there to be used.

When the bits and pieces long forgotten suddenly float up to the surface, it is called *inspiration*.

Ezra Jack Keats, in relating how he put together his Caldecott-winning book, *A Snowy Day,* once said that he saved patterned pieces of wrapping paper that fascinated him, old *Life* Magazine color pages that caught his eye, bits of material, sections of colored cloth. And one day these bits and pieces resolved themselves into the bright collages that became *A Snowy Day*. Ezra Jack Keats literally used the contents of a scrap basket, tranforming them with the glue and stickum of his own imagination into the story of a little boy and his adventures in the snow.

Writer's magic and creative memory

Not quite so literally, the writer performs this same kind of magic.

The following two examples show how my own scrap basket has worked. They illustrate what creative writing teachers *really* mean when they say: "Write about what you know." My books include stories about witches and princesses, seal-boys and lady pirates, giants and mandarins and seventeenth-century English mystics. I have never met any of them personally. But I know them, really know them, in the way that counts: In terms of my "creative memory"— that part of me that embroiders each of my personal experiences, transmuting them into fantasy or fiction—I know all these characters very well. And all the faraway places I write about are really home.

The Emperor and the Kite came from a single sentence I first saw in a lot of research I was doing on kites. Kite research is a way of life in our family. My father (who is the International Kite Flying Champion) and I have written five kite books and a dozen or more kite articles between us.

In 1961, while I was looking up some historical anecdotes about Chinese kites for the first of the books, I came upon a gigantic work entitled *Science and Civilization in China*. Buried in a paragraph in volume 2 was the sentence: "Emperor Shun was rescued by his daughter from a tower prison by means of a kite." Some five years later, this sentence floated up one day and pushed itself back into my consciousness. I wondered how the princess could have done such a thing—and why. Before I could stop myself, I was beginning to write a story about a princess so small and ill-thought of —when she was thought of at all—that she played in a corner of the palace garden by herself with only a kite for company. Princess Djeow Seow did not look very much like my father —though he is small, too—but her love of kites bore a striking resemblance to his. It all began with that snippet of a sentence, and it ended happily ever after when the book became a Caldecott Honor Book in 1968.

That same process of inspiration, or scrap-basketing, went to work on a folk song I had known for many years. The song, "The Great Selchie of Sule Skerry" (Child's *English and Scottish Popular Ballads*, 113) I had first learned as a twelve-year-old child. It tells the tale of a classic case of mismating—the coupling of a seal-man and an "earthly nourice," a human woman. It ends tragically and magically and is as dour and haunting as only an ancient Scots ballad can be. Hardly the stuff of a young children's book.

Some fifteen years after I first heard that song, my creative memory began to work on one of the verses:

> I am a man upon the land,
> I am a selchie in the sea.
> And when I'm far frae every strand,
> My dwelling is in Sule Skerry.

What if a selchie, a seal-man, was adopted into a human family? Would they try to keep him a man upon the land? Would they let him go back into the sea? I had that problem in mind when I began the story of *Greyling* in which a fisherman and his wife decide to bring up a seal pup they find stranded in the shallows—a seal pup that turns into a human baby when it is on the land.

That story began with a folk song, but I drew the country-side where it was set from a camping trip my husband and I had taken on the Pembroke Coast in Wales. The steep cliffs, the churning blue-green sea were in the scrap basket of my mind. They were all there when I needed them to make my word collage. Such scraps can be used again and again. The selchie reappeared in "The White Seal Maid," a story I wrote for my collection, *The Hundredth Dove,* and the great selchie himself became a major character in "Sule Skerry," a story in my young adult collection, *Neptune Rising.*

Idea file

There are times, of course, when inspiration gets a bit sluggish, like a car that needs extra choke on cold days, so one's creative memory occasionally can use some help. To this end, I insist that any writer—beginning or otherwise— keep an IDEAS file. Write down that snippet of a sentence if you like it and shove it into the file. Preserve that folk song verse in the Manila folder for a cold day.

Something special to keep in your IDEAS folder is a title list. Occasionally I sit down at the typewriter and devote half an hour or so just to writing down titles. It is a word-association game. And it is always helpful. The following is a title list I jotted down one day in 1962:

> *The Heart Wind*
> *Gomer the Rat King*
> *The Sea Witch*
> *A. Dragon & Son*
> *Rent-a-Dragon*
> *Dragon or Dragoon*
> *The King with Too Many Crowns*
> *The Waxworks Mouse*
> *The Man Who Grew Flowers in His Hair*

Let me tell you what has happened to those titles since. *The Heart Wind* became *The Girl Who Loved the Wind.* From that original title, an image of a wind-loving girl or a girl loving the wind came to my mind. From the image grew a whole story.

Gomer the Rat King became the villain of an easy reader, *Mice on Ice.*

The Sea Witch's opening sentences became incorporated into the opening of *Greyling.* The Sea Witch herself became a major figure in my fantasy novel, *The Magic Three of Solatia.*

All the dragon ideas, with the exception of the dragon who became the main actor in a story, "The King's Dragon," are still simply titles, as is *The King with Too Many Crowns.* *The Waxworks Mouse,* about a rodent who lives at Madame Tussaud's, is only three pages long. It may never be finished. And *The Man Who Grew Flowers in his Hair* was co-opted by *The Girl Who Cried Flowers,* which is the title story in a collection of the same name.

So, if anyone tells me that it is useless to brainstorm titles or to put snippets of sentences into my IDEAS file, I don't listen. I know better. From one hour's work has come twenty years' worth of inspiration.

You see, most people think of scrap baskets as receptacles for outworn or unwanted items. I come from a family of string-savers. As a string-saver in a kite-flying family, I know full well the value of bits and pieces of string. On the ground, the knots look crude, the string covered with old jam or crayons. But in the air, the string guides the kite into dips and soars, and helps the kite move with a grace that belies its crude origins.

Connecting "was" and "could be"

That, then, is where inspiration comes from, from the

scrap basket of your brain, the sum and total of all your experiences. And if you are lucky, those flashes of inspiration, those connections your brain makes between the *was* and the *could be,* will occur when you are comfortably seated in front of your typewriter and reams of paper by your side.

But what about the times you are driving sixty miles an hour down the highway or you're washing your hair or are in conference with the president of a rival corporation?

Those are the times that try your patience, test your mettle, and prove the worth of the fifteen-cent notebook. Your best friend—dearer to you than any lover or husband or wife or grandmother or cut-rate butcher—is that pocket-size notebook with an attached pen. That notebook is where you can scrawl the first words to a new mystery novel, for example, as I did when I pulled off the highway during a snowstorm. On the car radio, I had heard an advertisement for a fence that was, in the announcer's best New England accent, "horse-high, hog-tight, and bull-strong." It was too good to lose, and so I scribbled it on my notebook pages. The words sparked something in me, and so I added a few more lines which became the first paragraph of *The Inway Investigators:*

What makes a good fence? Grandad used to say being "horse-high, hog-tight, and bull-strong." And Uncle Henry, my guardian, winks and says, "Good neighbors make good fences." Only when I ask him what he means by that, he just laughs and says I'll understand in a while.

If I had waited until I'd reached home, undressed the baby, made myself a cup of tea, and gone to the typewriter, I would never have remembered that advertisement correctly. (Was it cow-tall? Bull-moose? Pig-smelly?) But I got it down right when I heard it, at the very moment it jolted something in me. When I returned home, I needed only to pop the scribble into my IDEAS file for future reference.

Of course, if no notebook is handy, scraps of paper, backs of envelopes, or paper napkins will do. As a youngster, I once had dinner with my father and the fabulous fantasy writer Gerald Kersh at a highly respectable New York restaurant. In the middle of a conversation, Kersh got this strange expression in his eyes, reached into his pocket for a pen, and started writing on the tablecloth. At dinner's end, my father picked up the check but Kersh paid for the tablecloth and took it home—presumably for *his* file.

Notebooks and files, then, are the perspiration that goes with inspiration. They serve another purpose as well. One of the problems of a fertile mind is that ideas and characters and plot crowd into it and clamor for expression. It is the author's responsibility to pick out the one still small voice amongst the many. The notebook, then, can become the repository of the many ideas and characters and plots. Time itself will help the author choose from among the plethora of viable ideas.

Buffon, the French naturalist, once contended that genius is simply a long patience. Part of any writer's long patience could be documented from his Manila folder labeled IDEAS or the notebook crammed with titles, snippets of sentences, and interesting quotes.

Marketability

There is a third step after inspiration. If the first step is the clicking together of the *was* and *could be,* and the second the long patience of notebooks and files, the third is the ofttimes dull research into marketability. Not marketability so that you know what to write. No one—and certainly no publisher—should tell you *what* to write. But once you have written a book or have an idea so spectacular you are going to write it come-what-may, you should have some notion of the marketability of your manuscript.

Publishers' catalogues provide a good shortcut. Each publishing house produces a catalogue of its current books and its past or backlist books. Simply by writing to the publisher you can request a catalogue of their juvenile books.

The catalogues are free; they are complete; and they are a gold mine of information. The catalogues will tell you what kinds of books the particular publishing company is interested in—fantasy, folk tales, nonfiction, sports, religious. It will give you an idea of the size of the list a company publishes per season: five to ten a season is small (Bradbury, Warne, Holiday House, Philomel, Knopf, Crown); over twenty-five is large (Harper & Row, Doubleday, Franklin Watts). Publishers' catalogues will tell you if there are series that might overlap your interests or books published recently that cover the same ground. A publishing company that has just produced a biography of John Kennedy or a book on kites or a novel about the Depression or a picture book on the changing seasons is not likely to do a similar one immediately. However, just because a publisher has done a fantasy book starring a mouse or a picture book about a girl in nursery school does not rule out their bringing out your fantasy about a shrew or your picture book about a boy in kindergarten. In studying catalogues, you must use common sense.

Publishers' catalogues are not the only shortcuts, however. Several magazines are useful, too. Most libraries will have *The Horn Book, Publishers Weekly, School Library Journal, Children's Literature in Education, Parent's Choice, Language Arts,* and *The Writer.*

The Horn Book is the only magazine that is for and about children's books. It comes out six times a year and is chock full of reviews, articles, and publishers' ads. If, in the words of one critic, it is occasionally full of "self-congratulatory prose," it is still the most important magazine for anyone in the field. And, if the only rule I insist on for the writing of children's books is the reading of them, then reading *The Horn Book* is a necessary corollary.

Both *Publishers Weekly* and *School Library Journal* contain short reviews of children's books each issue. The former is, as its name implies, a weekly magazine. Twice a year *PW* devotes an entire issue to children's books. The magazine is really a trade journal for the publishing world. Its reviews try to give the bookseller some indication of the appeal certain books will have for his customers.

It is important for anyone in the children's book field to know that bookstore sales are a very small part of children's book sales. Most children's books—70% is the conservative figure usually quoted, though some editors feel it is closer to 90%—are sold to the schools and libraries, rather than in bookstores. A quick glance at any royalty report will confirm this. The reason for this is that with picture books costing an average of eight to twelve dollars, most parents will pass up a book for a cheap doll or a gimmicky toy.

No wonder, then, that juvenile editors pay close attention to the reviews in *School Library Journal*. So should a novice writer. See which books are given starred reviews, *SLJ*'s highest accolade. Find those books in your own library and read them for yourself. Then you can begin to judge the standards by which *SLJ* makes its choices. The articles in *SLJ* are often highly technical library pieces, filled with library school jargon about access and rotation and filing systems, but occasionally a glimmer of something special for a writer can be found.

In almost every issue of *The Writer*, a monthly magazine devoted to helping beginning authors, there is an article by a well-known writer of children's books on the craft of writing. The magazine also includes marketing news, which is extremely helpful when you are at that stage in your work, for the needs of children's book publishers are listed annually in a special issue, and the market lists are updated regularly. Another excellent source of information is the Children's Book Council, 67 Irving Place, New York, New York 10003. Their monthly "Calendar" is a gold mine of assorted trivia, the kind of trivia that often sits for a year or so in a file and then sprouts inspirational wings. CBC, the parent council for all children's book publishers, sponsors Book Week, keeps a collection of every single new children's book in its New York office, and in general keeps tabs on everything that is happening in the field. It is a national clearing house, and any unanswered and seemingly unanswerable questions you may have on children's books can be directed to CBC.

If you are not acquainted with that old stand-by *Books in Print*—every library owns one—now is your time for greeting. *Books in Print* is the last word in ideas tried. If you think no one has ever written a book on African Water Skiing or a Child's Garden of Vegetables, or a fantasy novel about petrified forests, check it out in *Books in Print*'s subject matter index. *Books in Print* may tell you more than you want to know—including title, author, publisher, publication date, price, and subject matter.

Scheduling

Finally, there is the important matter of scheduling your writing time. You may find that you can average only one hour a day, or, as in the case of a friend of mine, from 8:30 in the morning until 6 in the evening, with a short lunch break at his desk. You may have as complicated a timetable as Phyllis A. Whitney's (she details it in her book, *Writing Juvenile*

Fiction) or as relaxed as mine. I keep no charts on my progress. I work as long as the words pour out, try a title list or two, and then quit if nothing more happens. But if you want to write, you will get to the pen or typewriter some portion of every day. If you are not really a writer, you will find any excuse to keep from writing. Or at least to keep from finishing what you have started to write.

Every month, I receive a letter or two from well-meaning acquaintances who want to know "How do you find time?" Then I sit down and look at what I have done lately: being a wife, raising three active youngsters, keeping house, teaching a writers workshop monthly and a course at Smith College weekly, chairing the trustees of my local library, reviewing books, coaching a high school team, not to mention frequent lectures at schools and libraries, clubs and conferences around the country. And I write back that I have plenty of time, what are they talking about? Because it really is not a question of *having* but of *making* time. Writing is not a matter of choice with me but of necessity. It is as necessary for me to give birth to a story when it is ready as it was for me to push out each of my three children when they were kicking to be born. If you don't have that natural drive to write, you are not and will not be a writer.

There you have a portrait of the artist as a young scrap heap. The head is inspiration. The midsection is perspiration. The feet are dedication. But if you are a storyteller, a real writer, these things will all become second nature to you, if indeed they are not already. And you can get down to the business and pleasure of learning about the many kinds of children's books and telling your own stories.

A picture is worth a thousand words.

—Old saying

Nothing lies like a picture.

—Old saying

3

Picture the Picture Book

WHEN A beginning writer thinks about the field of children's books, he or she is most likely to envisage a story with colored illustrations. When selecting a book as a gift for a child, a friend or relative probably thinks first of the beautifully illustrated picture book. When I mention to an acquaintance that I write for children, they often assume that I write stories with full-color illustrations.

Of course, picture books with color illustrations make up a large part of books published for children; almost half of my own children's books have been in this category. But when I look over my picture books, each is so different from its successor that I sometimes think the only relationship between one and another is that each has my name as author.

The category "picture book" is very broad. It touches

many different kinds of books. It will take at least two chapters even to begin to describe the many possibilities.

For example, the *picture story* is one kind of picture book. The *concept book* is another. The *ABC* is a third. The *folk tale* is a fourth. Each is a unique type of book, with its own particular problems, yet they all fall into the broad category of "picture book."

There are, in fact, only three things that can be said about writing picture books in general—and they are three warnings:

1. Be simple.
2. Understand structure.
3. Know the audience.

Two views

Essentially there are two views of a picture book. The first is that it is a palette with words. The second is that it is a story with illustrations. People who subscribe to the first view are artists. Most writers subscribe to the second.

Both are correct.

If you, the author, leave all the work in the picture book to an illustrator, you are giving away your creative part in the making of the story. On the other hand, if you do not leave something to the artist's imagination, you are usurping his role.

While the answer is "both," it leaves you, the author, with a difficult problem. You must walk the thin line between too much and too little. And like all tightrope walkers, you must make it look easy, look simple. Because SIMPLE is the operative word in writing a picture book.

A picture book is not a great opus or a large psychological novel or an intricately plotted mystery. In a picture book a writer must deal with one idea at a time. If you have another idea—write another picture book.

But simple does not mean slight. A full-bodied text can be simple. For example, *Peter Rabbit* by Beatrix Potter is a simple picture story about a naughty rabbit who, despite his mother's warnings, goes into the farmer's garden. He spends the rest of the book trying to escape. It is simple but not (as are many stories today) simple-minded. It has action, suspense, drama, several full-bodied characters, and an outcome that is always in doubt. After all, Peter's father had been made into rabbit pie by that same farmer. There is always the chance that Peter, who resembles his father in impetuousness, may end up in that same gruesome dish. That is why *Peter Rabbit* endures. It is simple—but not slight. And please notice the wonderfully distinctive words Beatrix Potter uses—not simple at all: exert, scuttered, camomile.

A final word about this idea of SIMPLE. As the poets know, the simplest things are often the hardest to do. Because picture books are so small, each word must count. No sloppiness of diction, no stray adjectives, no extra ideas. A picture book is really a kind of poem and should be treated as such.

An example from the opening paragraph of my book *Greyling* will give you an idea how each sentence must be polished. Words are substituted, changed, inserted until each line seems right.

Version #1:

THE SEA WITCH

Once on a time when wishes were aplenty, a fisherman and his wife lived in a hut beside the sea. They had all that they could eat that came out of the sea. Their hut was covered with the finest sea mosses that kept them cool in the summer and warm in the winter. They ate at a driftwood table and filled the house with sea pansies and seaweeds. There was nothing they needed or wanted—except a child.

Version #2:

SILKY

Once on a time when wishes were aplenty, a fisherman and his wife lived in a hut by the side of the sea not far from town. All that they could eat came out of the sea. Their hut was covered with the finest mosses that kept them cool in the summer and warm in the winter. Sea weeds and grasses grew in gay-colored pots by the windows and doors. And there was nothing they needed or wanted—except a child.

Final version:

GREYLING

Once on a time when wishes were a-plenty, a fisherman and his wife lived by the side of the sea. All that they ate came out of the sea. Their hut was covered with the finest mosses that kept them cool in the summer and warm in the winter. Seaweeds and grasses grew by the door. And there was nothing they needed or wanted except a child.

In this instance I was lucky. It took me only three tries to get the first paragraph. But whenever I begin a picture book, I remind myself of Blake's poem:

> Tiger! Tiger! burning bright
> In the forests of the night,
> What immortal hand or eye
> Could frame thy fearful symmetry?

What could be simpler than those four lines? It took Blake only *seven* revisions to make the poem that simple!

Structure

If *simple* is the first thing you must keep in mind when writing a picture book, the second is *structure*. The picture book is more structurally limited than any other kind of children's book. First there are page limits. A picture book is almost always either 32 or 48 printed pages long. Not all of that is text and/or illustration.

If you make a "dummy" for yourself, that is, staple together a blank "book" containing 32 pages (counting each side of the paper as an individual page) and another containing 48 pages, you will begin to understand the structural dimensions of a picture book.

Now number the pages consecutively and turn through these pages slowly. The first six to eight pages are "front matter"—half title, title page, copyright page, dedication if any. Sometimes these various pages will be elaborately illustrated; other times they will be in simple type. Check your mock-up against several different published picture books. See how they each differ. Some have two half-title pages, some include dedications on copyright pages, some have many extra blank pages.

It is very important that a beginning picture book writer understand the page limitations of a picture book. The number of pages is set because of the way a book is produced—sixteen pages to a "signature." The amount of front matter varies, but certain things *must* appear—the book's title, the copyright, the company's name. By law the copyright is on the reverse of the title page or on the title page. The title page usually includes, in addition to the title, the name of the author, illustrator, and publishing company. Certain things, therefore, are constant.

Make the structure of a picture book part of your visceral knowledge. Then you can stop thinking about it consciously when you write.

If you are aware of the structural limitations of a picture book before you write, two things will happen. First, you will not create a "tween" book, a book that falls between a picture book and an older book. And second, knowing the limits, you can then creatively stretch them.

Part of understanding a picture book's structure is understanding the role that art plays in it. A picture book is, after all, at least one-half art. Its distinction as a genre lies in the fact that on each page there is text *and* picture. (Occasionally there are picture books that have one page of text, one page picture; some that are pictures with no text at all. But for a basic definition, my statement stands.) So, as an author, you must be aware of the large role the artist plays in your picture book.

Remember: picture books should be the fusion of two artists—author and illustrator. They must complement one another, not be at war.

Since 1872, when a London printer named Edmund Evans invented the first full-color printing process, this war has been going on. (Aided and abetted, I may add, by the Caldecott Medal which is given to the "most distinguished picture book" each year—and awarded, significantly, to the artist, not the author of the book!)

Some illustrators believe, as Caldecott-winner Beni Montresor does, that "It is the image to which we most naturally respond." Or they follow art critic James Johnson Sweeney's dictum: "A child's book is essentially a work of visual art." But such pronouncements ignore the fact that many prize-winning books have been read over the radio or enjoyed in Braille editions by blind children.

The danger is always in over-illustrating. An excellent description of an overly-illustrated picture book is Louis Slobodkin's amusing example, "chilled lime gelatin, garnished with brilliant little bits of pimento—nestling in a few leaves of lettuce and tenderly resting on nothing." It is something for both the author and illustrator to beware—the Lime Gelatin Effect.

A fine artist sees the relationship of words and pictures

as the fusion of talents it should be. His perception lets him see the heart of a book, and he pictures what is on the paper and what is implied. He realizes exactly what another Caldecott winner, Uri Shulevitz, was saying when he wrote: "I try to see the images contained in the words of the story and to 'listen' to the different pictorial elements and their impact. . . ." In fact, my favorite description of the illustrator's role was Ed Young's, when he explained what he did before even beginning the Persian miniatures for my book, *The Girl Who Loved the Wind*: "I had to try to tune into the source of Jane's inspiration. I had to see with her eyes. Only when I was sure that was what I was doing, did I start to sketch."

Mental pictures

Since you as the author are seeking a fusion of text and pictures, it puts a special burden upon you, when you are writing a picture book, to keep pictures in your head. What you write must be illustratable. This means action is the most important thing, not the thoughts in your characters' heads. Psychological details are not easily illustrated; lots of conversation is not easily illustrated; long stretches of poesy for poesy's sake are not easily illustrated. But action is.

Yet while you keep the idea of pictures in your head, you should not write copious instructions to your illustrator. One of the most easily recognizable traits of the amateur author is a manuscript filled with parenthetical instructions to an artist.

For example, if you wrote the following, an editor would know immediately that you are a novice:

Once upon a time there lived a witch at the bottom of the sea. (Picture: witch in regular black witch's outfit and pointed hat and a mermaid's tail, sitting on a sunken ship's prow. Her hair is spun out by the ocean, a starfish nestles in the strands of her hair.)

The text itself should convey all that is in the parenthesis —if it is important. If it is not, then the author has to trust the artist's ability as he trusts his own. In other words, if you want to make sure your witch looks that way, you begin:

> Once on a time, when the world was filled with wishes the way the sea is filled with fishes, there lived a witch at the bottom of the sea. She wore a black dress that almost covered her scaly tail. And when she sat on a barnacled prow deep under the sea, singing up bubbles and letting the waves comb out her hair, starfish would come and settle in her curls.

Otherwise, you just write "Once upon a time there lived a witch at the bottom of the sea," and take your chances. Perhaps the artist will give her a starfish buckle on her hat. And maybe he'll draw her perched on a pirate's sunken treasure chest. But those are good ideas, too, and perhaps better than the ones you had originally dreamed.

The only time parenthetical advice to an illustrator is warranted is for a book in which the action of the story is —for the sake of humor or satire—exactly opposite the meaning of the words.

For example: "It was one of Thomas' *good* days. (Ill. Thomas is sitting under a pile of his toys, roller skates on his feet. He has obviously just slid into the pile.)" Even then, the text should be strong enough in the long run to indicate your true meaning. Besides, in your mind's eye you may be seeing Thomas as a little boy, the illustrator drawing a mouse child in roller skates, and the editor suggesting that, since there are already two mouse stories on her list that season, the artist should draw a skunk child instead.

So, while you should keep illustrations in mind in order to keep your writing sharp and spare, simple and direct, you should not have to give involved instructions to the artist. Here is a good, general rule: Strike out all instructions to the artist.

To reiterate, then, the picture book is a generic term for books that are at least one-half picture, one-half text. It is important to be simple and to understand the picture book's individual structure.

The age for these books is variously put at 3–7, 4–7, K–3 (Kindergarten through third grade) or pre-primer. That should not concern you as you write. Labeling the correct age for a book is the province of the editor and the sales staff. Your task is to write.

Small tales

One of the most common kinds of picture book is the *storybook*.

The storybook tells a small tale in a few words. It is simple —but not simple-minded. Fairly direct, it usually has a small cast of characters, and runs no longer than fifteen typewritten pages. (The shorter, the better.)

The storybook can be as modern and realistic as *Mama One, Mama Two*, by Patricia MacLachlan; *A Snowy Day*, by Ezra Jack Keats; *William's Doll*, by Charlotte Zolotow; or *The Dead Bird*, by Margaret Wise Brown. It can take place in the past like Brinton Turkle's tale of a little Nantucket Quaker lad, *Obadiah the Bold*, or Donald Hall's *Ox-Cart Man*, about an old-fashioned New England farm. The story can be full of magic or mystery or nonsense.

Selma Lanes, in her excellent critical essays in *Down the Rabbit Hole*, has written of picture stories: "The modifier 'literary' is best omitted from this experience, for the contemporary picture book is most clearly understood when viewed as a kind of halfway house between the seductions of TV, film or the animated cartoon and the less blatant charms of a full page of text." Certainly the picture book has been beaten almost to death by less than "literary" talents. But if you think of a storybook as an extended prose poem or a modern day campfire story, then you see it in perspective. There is no reason a good picture book cannot be as "literary" as Mrs. Lanes desires. It is only the bad story, the poorly written one, the text that is merely caption-writing, that fits Mrs. Lanes' harsh description.

A frequent problem that new picture story writers have is tension. A picture book plot should be like a hill with a path leading straight to the top, as the problem (plot) progresses. The high point of the hill is the climax. The end of the book should be just a short drop down. Too much meandering, and you lose your reader. Too many stray, unrelated incidents, and the young listener will leave your lap. The line of the picture book plot should be taut.

Perception books

The *concept book,* as its name implies, is a book that deals with ideas, concepts, large-scale problems in a small-scale way.

In a sense, concept books are gimmick books. They explore an idea, a concept, in an unusual manner. Hopefully, in a manner which will both teach and amuse.

Think of an idea: what is time? what is rain like? what can you do with a pocket? where do animals sleep? what can you do with mud? what are good manners? what is snow and what is fog?

There are already some excellent books about these concepts. Phyllis McGinley did a book about time in rhyme. *Rain Rain Rivers* is a sensitive tone poem by Uri Shulevitz.

Eve Merriam wrote a poetic picture book that asks: "What oh what can you do with a pocket?/Take it and shake it and see . . ." In *Where Do Bears Sleep?* by Barbara Shook Hazen, a child can learn that animals sleep in pens and dens, in caves, on rafters and roofs, and in holes, among other places. There is a book by Byrd Baylor called *Everybody Needs a Rock,* which tells the reader, in sensitive, cadenced prose, about rocks—and about the difference between aloneness and loneliness. No one has yet written a better manners-for-kids book than Sesyle Joslin's *What Do You Say, Dear?* and *What Do You Do, Dear?* And Alvin Tresselt's prose poems, *White Snow, Bright Snow* and *Hide-and-Seek Fog,* with Roger Duvoison's glowing pictures, are already classics of children's literature.

Just because an idea, a concept, has already been explored by one writer does not put it off limits to another. As there are supposed to be only ten basic plots in the world, so there are probably a small finite number of concept book ideas. What makes the concept book original is the author's handling.

For example, the difference between big and little has been explored in at least four books by such different authors as Leonore Klein (*Tom and the Small Ant*), Kazue Mizumura (*The Way of an Ant*), Marcia Brown (Caldecott-winner *Once a Mouse*) and by me (*It All Depends*). The Klein book and my book are both in occasional rhyme and rhythmic prose. The Mizumura and Brown books are straight stories. The former is a more didactic tale about an ant that keeps climbing higher and higher flowers and trees in an attempt to reach the sky. The latter is a very spare, stark fable about an Indian hermit and a mouse. The four books are very different, yet each is exploring the same basic idea: what is big, what is little.

Concept books really began with Margaret Wise Brown

in the 1930s and her "awareness compositions," as educator May Hill Arbuthnot calls them. Miss Brown launched a seemingly endless line of these perception books. Her imitators became legion. By the 1950s, with schools and libraries demanding more and more of these pre-primary educational books, "It began to look," according to Miss Arbuthnot, "as if we were in for a kind of pernicious anemia of theme and plot, with language experience in place of stories, and pitter-patter in place of events." That anemia has cleared up. The concept books being demanded by editors today must be full-bodied books, not just pitter-patter educational experiences. But the demand does continue.

The demand continues because not only editors and librarians want these books. Children do, too. The concept book helps them explore something they feel is worth exploring. It gives them a handle on an idea. The concept book is a child's mnemonic device. It is conscious language play, and children adore language. They have much more fun with it than we staid adults, who feel it should be used for communicating important ideas—immediately.

It is important that you have fun in a concept book. However, be wary of rhyme, which, unless handled extremely well, becomes mere doggerel. Be especially careful if you are one of those writers who claims, "But rhyme comes so easily to me. I write verse at the drop of a strophe." The very facility with which you rhyme may prove your downfall. Try exploring rhythmic prose instead, prose that sometimes rhymes, that almost rhymes, that occasionally rhymes, or uses internal or slant rhyme. This kind of approach to rhyme can work very well with picture books and, especially, concept books.

Here are two examples of occasional rhyme that get away from the bumpety-bump of doggerel.

From my own concept book, *See This Little Line?*:

Or put your line
On top of mine
And we can, indeed can
        make a snow man or a tin can
           or a toucan.
Two can.
Who can?
You can,
    I can,
      We can.

And from Eve Merriam's *Small Fry,* which is a concept book about the generic names for the young of various animal species:

Here comes the cub parade,
Cubs that doze and cubs that roar.
    Bear cubs
        lion cubs
Cubs that flip and cubs that nip.
Seal cubs
    shark cubs
        tiger cubs
           fox cubs
             leopard cubs
             otter cubs.
What are not cubs.

In a concept book you must stick to a simple idea and expand on it. In music this is known as a "riff" or "variations on a theme." Think of concept books as riff books. Embroider the original idea, play around with it, have a good time. But do not stray from one simple idea to another simple idea. That suddenly makes a simple book much too complex to work.

The concept book will probably be shorter in manuscript

than a picture story book. While the picture story books runs up to fifteen pages, a concept book should remain below ten typewritten pages. *See This Little Line?* was two typed pages long, 408 words arranged in short poetic lines. *It All Depends* was longer in manuscript—five typewritten pages. In such a small space you only have time to work on one simple idea.

Alphabet books

One kind of picture book that seems easiest to write but is probably the single most difficult to write well is the alphabet book. Writing one of these is not as simple as ABC!

I have attempted any number of alphabet books myself: an urban ABC, a pirate ABC, a girl's-name ABC. Even after the birth of my first child, a new-mother's ABC.

I failed every time.

As an editor, I read alphabet book attempts at least twenty times a week. It is the kind of book most attempted by novice writers. It is also the one form upon which the most indignities have been visited.

Not only novice writers, but professionals as well "commit" abortive ABCs. As a book reviewer, I have been sent a number of ABCs that fall below the line of critical applause into the well of critical catcalls.

From the 1800s version of *A–Apple Pie* by Kate Greenaway through Edward Lear's funny phonetic nonsense alphabet, Wanda Gág's *ABC Bunny*, Garth Williams' colorful *Big Golden Animal ABC* to the wildly colorful *Wildsmith's ABC* by Brian Wildsmith, the best authors and illustrators have tried their hand at alphabet books. Yet most have failed. The really good alphabet books—including the ones just mentioned above—can be counted on the fingers of two, at the most three, hands. And that after almost five centuries of alphabet rhymes. (Mayster Benet, rector of Sandon in

Essex, England, is sometimes cited as the first writer of alphabet books. He composed an ABC rhyme in 1440.)

Why are alphabet books so enduring, so popular—and so difficult? They are enduring and popular because they seem the perfect beginning book and offer such a variety of objects and ideas for the youngest readers.

But difficult? The answer to that is that alphabet books are anomalies. They are trying to teach the reader using as tools that which they are trying to teach; to be exact, using words which, since the "reader" does not yet know the alphabet, he or she simply can't read.

This is why the illustrators come out much the best in the battle of the ABC book.

The simplest ABCs—and to many minds the best—are the ones that show the letters of the alphabet one by one and have a large, easily-identifiable object representing the letter. A for apple, B for ball, and nothing else. No need for a writer at all. The artist's interpretation of each object provides the book's distinction and originality.

Yet if an alphabet book is not to be just a collection of bright pictures held together by the ABCs, pearls on the strand of an artist's genius, there must be something further to hold the jewels all together. This is where a writer comes in: to provide an idea, a theme, something upon which to hang the entire alphabet.

For example: *An ABC of animals.* Roger Duvoisin's *A for the Ark,* uses both the Biblical tale and a whole alphabet of animals—two by two.

An ABC of city sights and sounds. Phyllis McGinley's *All Around the Town* in sprightly verse, wittily combines letters and sounds: "V is for the Vendor/a very vocal man. . . ."

An ABC of working people. A beautiful old favorite of mine is an ABC from 1850, *Alphabet of Trades,* in which "M begins Milliner so fine,/And Miner, working in a Mine,/

And for Merchant, with his store, trading to a foreign shore."

Or you might try any of the following: a hospital ABC, a things-on-wheels ABC, a Halloween ABC, an under-the-Christmas-tree ABC, a garden ABC, a kings and queens ABC, an American ABC, a black history ABC, an Indian tribes ABC, a feminist ABC, a country mouse and city mouse ABC, an eating ABC, a bird-watcher's ABC, etc.

The children's room of your local library is a repository of themes tried. It is definitely the place to visit before you attempt to develop a theme of your own. Give your book a most thorough "library test," for there is nothing more discouraging than a rejection letter that says: "While this is delightful, it is too similar to. . . ."

Once you have a theme, give your idea the "X Test." An alphabet book stands or falls on its most difficult letters. These are, ordinarily, X, J, Q, and Z. (Of course not all these are actually the most difficult in every case. For example, in my pirate alphabet, X marks the spot on the treasure map, J is for jewels, but K is a doozy!) The X Test is the most valuable way to weed out absolutely unworkable ABC ideas.

If your X or Q or J or Z is far-fetched or only vaguely relevant to the theme of the book, throw it out. And if you can find nothing better for the letter, throw out that theme, too.

I once had a perfectly marvelous idea for an alphabet book I called *A, B, A Building I See.* It was to be about the building of a skyscraper, and each letter was to demonstrate a step in the process. A for the architect who begins the building the way A begins the alphabet—all the way through X on the new panes of glass to keep people from putting their hands through. I even consulted a close cousin of mine who is a New York City architect and "knows things." However, instead of giving my book the X Test, I just plunged into writing it. I devised a sprightly rhyme for each of the letters in turn and spent weeks polishing each couplet. I sailed through one letter after another until I came to Y and Z and—oops. All I could come up with was Y for Yardstick and Z for Zinc with which the iron girders are dusted. With a large mental gulp, I finished the book on that weak note and sent it out. After a number of nice, polite, helpful rejection letters, the perfectly marvelous idea joined any number of others in my dead manuscript file.

It was then I devised the X Test.

However, if you have a theme that is original enough to pass the library test and broad enough to pass the X Test, then plunge into your alphabet book.

An alphabet book may be in rhyme or in prose. It can be serious or funny. It may be illustrated by drawings or photographs. But as with all picture books, *it must be simple.* It is, more than other concept books, a book for non-readers. While a number of ABC books may have been published using enormous words and complicated actions (Dahlov Ipcar's *I Love My Anteater with an A,* or Peggy Parish's *A Beastly Circus*), books that use words like xenophobia or names like Xerxes or Xanthippe are begging the alphabet question. They are for adults, not children.

The audience

Which in a very roundabout way brings us to the third and final basic warning about picture books in general: *Know the audience.*

Who is the audience—adults or children?

Remember this simple truth about picture books: they must appeal to both the reader and the read-to. After all, it is the reader—not the read-to—who does the book buying. How many preschoolers sit in a Madison Avenue office with the budget of a publishing company in one hand, a blue pencil in the other? How many pre-primary children are given eight to ten dollars and are allowed to go to the local bookstore to purchase their own books? How many under-sixes do the book selecting and buying for the local library? Children, the read-to's, are the great silent majority of the reading world. Their only veto is not to listen. The vocal minority consists of mothers and fathers, teachers, librarians, grandparents— the readers—the ones with money. To get to the silent majority, you have to appeal to the vocal minority first.

Does this sound cynical? It is not meant to be. For if you have never been an adult reading a bad ABC or simpleminded picture story about Polly Parakeet Ties Her Shoes over and over to a favorite child, you cannot know the dark night of the soul when you have to resort to "Let's watch the TV" just to get that awful book off your lap at last. Some children *can* stand multiple readings of a bland or uninteresting book because of the cuddling that goes with reading. Reading to a child is a tactile entertainment. It excites more than just the ear and eye. So a child who craves attention would just as readily listen raptly to a complete rendition of the Brooklyn telephone book.

The children in the audience do not lack judgment. They are excellent critics, often quite brutally outspoken since they have not been "civilized" out of twitches, boos, and yawns. But a book is more than a book to a child, and the writer of books for children must not ever forget that.

So, whenever faced with the question of *who is the audience,* I give this answer from C. S. Lewis: "I am almost inclined to set it up as a canon that a children's story which is enjoyed only by children is a bad children's story."

. . . certainly, so long as man exists, [fables]
can never perish.

—Nathaniel Hawthorne

4

Mining the Folk Lode

ONCE UPON a time, of course, there were no written stories,
no literary tales. But there were a lot of illiterate tales: bits
and pieces of legend, myth, history all twined together and
handed down father to son and mother to daughter. This
way of preserving ancient traditions has been called "a process of mouth-to-mouth resuscitation."

The invention of the alphabet changed all that. Slowly all
the tales were put on rock or parchment or paper—whatever
was handy at the time. In committing these old tales to rock
or parchment or paper, something happened: Everything became more rigid. The older gods became more defined. People
began to believe that what was written was so and, conversely,
what was not written was not so.

Unfortunately, people still believe that what is written is
so. Especially in our favorite magazines and newspapers. An
argument ends when someone quotes *Time* or *Newsweek* the

way our forefathers quoted scripture. Sometimes it is difficult to find the kernel of truth that began the stories.

Where stories began

It is the same with folk tales. (Not that people believed entirely in giants and mermaids and fairies. There was always a modicum of disbelief in these tales. As J. R. R. Tolkien has written: "If men really could not distinguish between frogs and men, fairy stories about frog-kings would not have arisen.") Inside each of the old folk tales is a kernel of truth. And if you are a scholar and want to delve into who-is-the-real-King-Arthur and what-was-a-dragon-really and were-dugongs-the-real-mermaids, that is your prerogative. It is not necessarily important to the writing of fairy and folk tales to know *what* began the old stories; it is only necessary to know that a distorted truth was most often the beginning. As Dennis the Menace explains to his father in one of the cartoons, as he is sitting in the corner being punished, "I didn't fib! I made a *fable* like Aesop and those other guys!"

The old literature was told for and by a class of people "who have steeped everything in the heart; to whom everything was a symbol." Yeats, who retold some of the loveliest of the old Irish folk and fairy tales, wrote that. I believe that this is where the connection with writing such tales comes today. The "class" that these tales appeal to in the twentieth century are the young readers and those of us who, like children, still have everything steeped in the heart. We, the children and the childlike, look at a dugong and see a mermaid, glimpse a moth at dusk and see a newly released soul, and count all windmills as giants.

Writing stories today in the folk tale tradition, or writing fairy tales and picture books about magic, involves a process I call *mining the folk lode*. The writer has to draw upon the old sources either consciously or unconsciously, recreating subtly the atmosphere of the campfire around which each of these tales was told, the great hall where the hero songs were sung, or the nursery where the peasant nanny remembered out loud for the benefit of her young charges.

There are really three ways a writer can use folk material today, now that the tribal campfire, the great hall, and the nursery are gone. They are ways that recall each of these lost places.

As a writer, you may use the folk wisdom of the fantastics and fools that were found in the old stories, the giants and dragons of the old quest tales, or the fairies that once peopled the countryside of man's mind. You may restructure an old song, weaving the elements into a new tapestry. Or you may simply, like the nursery nanny, retell a tale heard in childhood, working your own magic and thus help change the material. This last is what scholars label "the folk process."

The nanny stories

Sometimes called "cottage tales," these are the dear familiar stories you may have learned directly from your parents' storehouse of stories or from the pages of a worn and well-beloved book. Stories like "The Three Bears" or "Sleeping Beauty" or "Little Red Ridinghood" can be found in many different versions. Folklorists call them "variants." "Cinderella," for example, has been traced from China to Peru with many stops in between. A study noted five hundred versions of the tale in Europe alone—which gives you a good idea of how often a basic story can be changed. For instance, the English Catskin manages to get dresses made of silver, gold, and feathers to entice her prince, but finally wins him through her wits. The Scots call their Cinderella Rushen Coatie, and her slipper, though magical and capable of jumping into the

prince's pocket by itself, is of good serviceable leather. The
glass slipper is a French invention, and probably a mistake
at that. The French word *vair* meaning fur and *verre* meaning
glass are pronounced alike, and it is more likely that the
original slipper was of fur and that something was lost (or
gained) in transcribing the story from oral to written form.

Retelling an old story is, from a writer's point of view, the
simplest use of folk material; yet it is not a simple thing to
do. I personally find it the least interesting of ways to utilize
folk material: old wine in new bottles. Still, if you are particu-
larly in love with an old tale, or want to practice the art of
folk-tale telling (and art it is), or if you are an artist who is
mainly interested in the illustrating and only secondarily concerned with writing a tale, you could do worse than to start
with an old tale. Beni Montresor, for example, used the Ros-
sini opera version of "Cinderella" and based his pictures on
the stage settings and costume designs he produced for the
Metropolitan Opera's production. The result was a book
worth looking at for the glowing pictures, as an example
of yet another version of an old tale.

The important thing about retelling an old tale is first to
get the story down pat and then to ignore the source. The
oldest sources are usually the most beautiful or poetic rendi-
tions of a tale. If you are interested in folk tales, at least some
of the following should be on your shelves: Yeats' *Irish Fairy
and Folk Tales*; a Victorian translation of *Grimm's Household Stories*; the Lady Charlotte Guest's classic telling of the
Welsh hero tales, *The Mabinogion*; the Peter Asbjörnsen and
Jörgen Moe collection of *Norwegian Folk Tales*; the Russian
collection of Asanyev; the English folk tales collected by
Joseph Jacobs; Frazer's *The Golden Bough*; Graves' *The
White Goddess*; a translation of *The Thousand and One
Nights*; and Willi Fehse's translation of *The Thousand and
One Days*. Some African collections and selected American

tall tales and American Indian legends will round out your folk shelf.

The older versions are closer to the oral tradition from which these tales sprang. Often the collector took these stories down straight from the mouths of the storytellers. If you read them, you will note the poetic style. These tales were meant to be heard. The word *tale* comes from the Anglo-Saxon *talu*, or speech. Tale is related to telling. So the tale as it is retold should be pleasing to the ear. Read each of your sentences aloud as you work. Pretend you are telling the story and then the tale will be readable. Sound is important. Said C. S. Lewis: "It is important to please the ear as well as the eye." If the original tales were meant to be heard, yours should do no less.

Here are the openings to two versions of a famous English folk tale. The first is from the original Joseph Jacobs version, first printed in 1898. The second is from a modern retelling. Both have a poetry in them. Try reading them out loud. Good poetry makes good drama. The best tales are full of both poetry and drama.

From *The Crock of Gold*, by Joseph Jacobs, pictures by William Stobbs (Follett):

> In the old days, when London Bridge was lined with shops from one end to the other, and salmon swam under the arches, there lived at Swaffham in Norfolk, a poor pedlar. He'd much ado to make his living, trudging about with his pack at his back and his dog at his heels, and at the close of the day's labour was but too glad to sit down and sleep. Now it fell out that one night he dreamed a dream, and therein he saw the great bridge of London town, and it sounded in his ears that if he went there he should hear joyful news.

And from *The Pedlar of Swaffham*, by Kevin Crossley-Holland (Seabury):

> One night John Chapman had a dream.

A man stood by him, dressed in a surcoat as red as blood; and the man said, "Go to London Bridge. Go and be quick. Go, good will come of it."

After you read some of the best of the collections you will see why retelling is not necessarily a simple thing to do. To do more than just a gimmicky or gimcrack job, the dedicated author should have some idea of the background of a legend or tale. Just as an illustrator knows costume and landscape of a period, the reteller must have such knowledge, too.

Barbara Cooney, when she retold and illustrated Chaucer's *Chanticleer and the Fox,* drew a raven sitting in one of the windows because in Chaucer's day a raven was an omen of ill-to-come. And all the flowers which she drew lovingly in the book grew in England when Chaucer was alive. Ms. Cooney has written that she did not expect every child—or even every adult—to catch these touches. But they help create a total world. If an illustrator takes that much time with a book, the author must, too.

Does this sound like too much work when all you want to do is simply retell an old folk tale? Books, even picture books, change lives. When you think of it that way, asking a little bit of homework from the author is not asking too much.

Great Hall stories

Let's move from the nursery out into the Great Hall. In the once-upon-a-time days, the noblemen and their ladies would listen to a wandering minstrel sing of great deeds, of grails sought after, dragons conquered, of battles fought, of maidens won. The modern writer can, like Tolkien or Lloyd Alexander, borrow these bardic elements and reshape them to his own use.

Tolkien, for example, made up Hobbits and Ents. But he borrowed Trolls and Elves. Yet in the process, the folk process, he gave back more than he took. His Lothlórien will forever be the place of elvish enchantment to anyone who reads *The Lord of the Rings.* Dragons will always sound a little like greedy Smaug in *The Hobbit.* Lloyd Alexander may have leaned heavily on the Welsh *Mabinogion* tales, but he created an Assistant Pigkeeper who will ride forever in a reader's mind like a lantern bearer for the older gods.

The Great Hall stories are usually quest tales in which a hero or heroine moves through one magical adventure after another in search of a reward, an enchanter or enchantment to break, a magic castle to discover, an evil ring/weapon to destroy. As such, the Great Hall tales need a larger scope, a mighty setting for their magic. Usually a novel-length book is the best way to explore these stories. (They will be discussed at length in the next chapter, on fantasy.)

The line between folk tale and fantasy is a fine one, a line that is crossed and recrossed at will. When a fantasy novel uses folk elements, or a folk tale is imbued with elements of a magical quest, the line disappears.

Certainly there are some dragons, trolls, and elves and the like depicted in smaller-scale books. *Everyone Knows What A Dragon Looks Like,* by Jay Williams; Tommie de Paola's *Helga's Dowry;* Raymond Briggs's *Jim and the Beanstalk* are examples. But the larger-than-life themes of the Great Hall tales, the stories of heroes and heroines on a heroic scale, are best dealt with in a novel.

Campfire tales

So we come to the campfire tales, the big catch-all. Basically, there are four kinds of campfire tales.

First are the *cumulative stories,* The House That Jack Built tales. These are stories that first spiral upward and then back downward to a conclusion. Such tales as "Johnny Cake," "Henny Penny," and "The Gingerbread Man" are tales that work marvelously with the very youngest listeners. The endless repetitions and the simplicity of the storyline catch up even the most inattentive little listeners until they find themselves telling the story along with the speaker. These are game-stories because the circular mode of the story invites participation. Just as the most popular songs with young children are game songs, and especially rounds which repeat and repeat, so too these stories are tales told in the round. Many of these stories work right into game situations in a classroom.

The second category is the *talking-animal tale*. Again, "Henny Penny" is a good example. So are "The Three Bears," "The Three Billy Goats Gruff," "The Three Little Pigs." What these stories have in common, besides the fact that the animals converse, is that they often teach a simple lesson. I would suggest, though, that you do not write your moral at the top of the page and then proceed with your tale—as a friend of mine does. These talking-animal stories are successful only if they are good fun to begin with.

You must be extremely careful of the talking-animal tales of the "Polly Parakeet Ties Her Shoes" type. It is neither folk tale nor fantasy. What it is, is "cute." Most editors abhor anthropomorphic stories. Even the best and most popular of authors has come a cropper on a talking-animal story; for instance, Elizabeth Bowen's *The Good Tiger* and Jose Aruego's *Pilyo the Piranha*. A good rule of thumb would probably be: If it is an animal, it shouldn't talk; if it is human, it shouldn't walk on all fours. (For more about talking animals, see chapter 8.) However, if against all warnings, you insist on writing a talking-animal story, you might try casting it in a folk tale mode, for, as everyone knows, in the once-upon-a-time days anything was possible.

The third category is the *silly tale*. In this type of story, the numskull or the stupid son (or daughter) does something so outrageous that you can't help laughing. For example, *Hee Haw* (Ann McGovern) is a modern version of the old Aesop fable, in which a man and his son want to trade their donkey at the fair but can't quite figure out how to get it there. A new retelling of the folk favorite, "The Husband Who Was to Mind the House," is *Turnabout* (William Weisner). It is a tale that, in these days of women's liberation, takes on added dimensions. Always in the midst of the playfulness of the silly tale there is a sense of pain. Slipping on a banana peel can look funny, but someone is likely to be hurt. The young listener can feel above the foolishness, can be aware of but not threatened by the pain. And the young reader also feels that he or she is smarter and superior to the ninnies he is reading about. In the old days, the downtrodden peasants made up these tales so that *they* could feel better and smarter than the ninnies. Children, one of the last of our downtrodden and unliberated minorities, feel the same. (And isn't that, in a sense, what much of vaudeville is about?)

In each of the above categories—the cumulative tales, the talking-animal stories, the silly tales—the problem with writing a "story in the manner of a folk tale," as the sales people are wont to say, or "literary folk tales," as the scholars put it, is to use the device without retelling an old story.

Here are some you might try:

*a modern setting of "The Gingerbread Man" using a pizza that escapes from the pie maker's hands and rolls out the door and down the street of a modern city. (See also, *The Elephant and the Bad Baby,* by Elfrida Vipont, as an excellent example of the modern use of a cumulative device.)

* three sparrows talk of the coming winter, and fly to three separate houses where they are greeted in three different ways. (See also, *Has Winter Come?* by Wendy Watson, for a delightful example of a talking-animal tale.)

*a man decides to build a tall apartment building and uses the wrong tool each step of the way, on the advice of all the "sidewalk superintendents." (See also, Judith Barrett's *Old MacDonald Had An Apartment House.*)

The fourth and final category of the campfire stories is the magic tale: fairies and little people, witches and wizards, wise women and wise men, giants and ogres, magical animals and magical objects. All the trappings of enchantment. The magic tale is my personal favorite—both to read and to write. The trick is to *borrow* a bit of magic from an old tale and use it in a new way.

In writing *Greyling,* I borrowed a magical being, the selchie, sometimes seal and sometimes human, from Scottish legend. But the story is my own. Hans Christian Andersen borrowed the traditional half-woman, half-fish for his story, "The Little Mermaid." Richard Kennedy used the folk figure of Death, dressing him up as a New England C.P.A., in *Come Again In The Spring.* Modern folk tale creators are always borrowing. It is the borrowing that makes each of these *folk,* the telling that makes each a *tale.*

I have been criticized for not using working-class people in my stories—unless, of course, they marry the beautiful enchanted princess. Such critics do not understand the distinctive appeal that princesses and kings have for children. Children know these are pretend kings and make-believe princesses. But they do not mistake this fantasy for their own real lives. As C. S. Lewis says: "The fairy tale is accused of giving children a false impression of the world. . . . I think no literature gives them less of a false impression. . . . What profess to be realistic stories . . . are far more likely to deceive them."

The real and the magic

In writing folk tales, it is important to keep two things in mind. First, you must remember that the most unlikely things in modern life may be grist to your mill. Although you may not realize it at the time, elements of real life are always sneaking into the magic.

Here are two examples from my own books—and my own life—that illustrate what I mean.

In *The Boy Who Had Wings,* the Greek boy Aetos is never happy when he is different. Only after his wings fall off and he is able to live a "normal" life is he secure and pleased. Yet, years later, all the young people pray to the gods to send them such "blessed" children, children with great arching wings. Similarly did I feel out of place and unloved in college, with my long hair and my habit of writing poetry at all hours. Only now, I receive letters all the time from classmates who were never my friends, wanting to write themselves or hoping their own children are published some day. Thus, Aetos' story is, in a way, a version of my own life.

I began *The Bird of Time,* in which a miller's son discovers a bird that can marvelously control time, when I first discovered my mother was dying of cancer. Ostensibly, the book was started when I misheard the lyrics of a rock song on the car radio. I thought the words were "time bird," since the singers mumbled a lot. Before I had quite caught the real lyrics (which had nothing to do with either a bird or time), I found myself consciously thinking about a time bird. (Subconsciously, as I found out later, I was also thinking about the *Rubáiyát of Omar Khayyám* which my mother had given me when I was ten, which sings, "The Bird of Time has but a little way/ To fly—and Lo! the Bird is on the Wing." What could a time bird do, I wondered? Only after I finished the story and showed my mother the manuscript (she died before the book was published) and she said, "Intimations of mortality, eh?" did *I* realize what the book was about. I wanted to be able, like Pieter in the book, to manipulate time—to slow time down or stop it altogether in order to save my mother. In real life, I could not keep her forever; in the book, in another way, I could.

Structural elements and techniques

If you remember that anything can become part of your inspirational mechanism, then you can proceed to the second important thing to know about writing a folk tale. Know its structure.

A folk tale manuscript should run between five and fifteen pages, but the shorter the better. The age group that most appreciates the folk tale is 4 to 104. (The sales people, who are the most conservative members of a publishing house complex, will tell you it is 4 to 10.) However, do not worry about either the page or age limitations as you write. Consider them briefly as you revise. But remember, never try to second-guess an editor. I do not—and I have been an editor myself.

Some of the structural elements you should keep in mind are these: tag-openings, "and then," speed of plot.

Folk tales usually have a tag-opening, like the Persian "Once there was and there was not. . . ." You can either use the classic "Once upon a time . . ." or try to create your own opening in a style appropriate to your story. I have begun various tales like this: "Once on a time when wishes were a-plenty. . . ." "Once in the East where the wind blows gently on the bells of the temple . . ." "Once on the far side of yesterday . . ." "Once on the plains of Thessaly where horses grow like wheat in the fields. . . ." and (please forgive me) "Once upon a maritime. . . ."

The theme of a folk tale is usually apparent from its beginning. Keep in mind that it is a story, not a character development or a mood piece. These themes are never abstract but rather robust, easily understandable: earning a place in the world; seeking a fortune; escaping a powerful enemy; outwitting an evil opponent. Or the themes may be even more specific: bringing a donkey to the fair; marrying the Czar's daughter; getting safely through a dark forest.

Don't waste time. As they say in the modern spy dramas, *get in, get it over with, get out!* A key phrase to remember when working on a folk tale is *"and then . . ."* It will remind you of the breathless child at your elbow waiting to hear the rest of the story. In a folk tale, speed is of the essence. Speed is helped by an economy of words, fast action, an inventive plot, and a swift but satisfactory conclusion.

A good fairy story or folk tale must have a clear and uncluttered end. It does not have to be a *happy ending.* After all, Andersen's little mermaid dives back into the sea without her prince, and minus her tail and her tongue. But everyone and everything must be dealt with, in one way or another.

As for the characters, with all that plot and theme, there is not much time for full-bodied, in-depth portrayals. But folk tale characters tend to be types—the foolish son, the beautiful princess, the wicked giant, the wise old woman, the clever peasant. For the most part, the good are good and the evil are evil. One wins the prince or princess, the other wins his just deserts. Still, small touches can make the type-characters very individual. Beauty's absurd and constant longing for a rose in winter delivers her into the hands (the paws?) of the Beast. The third little pig's flat-footed burgher qualities make a house of bricks a totally consistent choice. Goldilocks' unthinking destruction of the bears' house indicates she has the attention span of a two-year-old, which is why she is so everlastingly popular with the threes and fours. They, solid elder citizens that they are, would never be like *that!* These individualizing touches added to types make up a portrait gallery of totally unforgettable characters.

That leaves only one more question to be answered. With all the delightful folk stories out of the oral tradition, and with all the marvelous stories transcribed by such inventive authors as Charles Perrault, why write new ones? Folk stories and fairy tales are a way of looking at life, and they carry important messages to the conscious, pre-conscious, and the unconscious mind. The noted child psychologist Bruno Bettelheim, in a fascinating book, *The Uses of Enchantment: The Meaning and Importance of Fairy Tales,* says, ". . . they offer new dimensions to the child's imagination, suggesting to him images with which he can structure his daydreams."

Fairy tales are important. The old tales—and the newly crafted ones, shaped from the waking dreams of literary men and women.

The new stories, if they are well told, are as valid as the old. The children are heirs to the three traditions: oral, transcribed, and literary tales. They do not distinguish between the origins for their enjoyment. A good story is a good story is a good story. As May Hill Arbuthnot wrote: "The distinction between the old folk tale and the modern fairy tale is of no importance to the child. Magic is magic to him, whether he finds it in Grimm, Andersen, or Dr. Seuss."

A fantasy story is a coded message to a child.
—Uri Shulevitz

5

There Would Be Unicorns

WHEN I was a child, I was a poet. When I grew up, I wrote fantasy. It seems a logical development, for fantasy is a logical extension of poetry.

Poetry expresses a unique way of seeing the world, and so does fantasy. Fantasy and poetry are natural for children. The world itself is new to them. A literature which celebrates newness is as natural to them as the world itself.

Speculative fiction

When I was in college, I wrote a poem that began: "There would be unicorns if I were God . . ." And though the poem was not about being a writer but about becoming a woman, whenever I think about being a writer, I think about the beginning of that poem. For a writer of any sort, but especially a writer of fantasy, is a kind of god. Out of nothing, or out of the chaos of his mind, the writer of fantasy creates a world and then peoples it.

Before proceeding further, however, let's define this word *fantasy*. It is a most elusive term, a wraith word.

First, some borrowed definitions: J. R. R. Tolkien, in a brilliant essay, "On Fairy Stories," says that fantasy involves the subcreative art, that it is a secondary world in which things happen "with arresting strangeness."

Eleanor Cameron, in *The Green and Burning Tree,* calls fantasy "the literature of magic," though she is quick to point out that this includes both good and bad.

May Hill Arbuthnot, in her *Children and Books,* defines fantasy more pedagogically as "a tale of magic, often beginning realistically but merging quickly into adventures strange, astonishing, and dreamlike."

And Tolkien quotes an acquaintance who called the making of fantasy stories "breathing a lie through silver."

But I would say it still differently. Perhaps because I am a science fiction buff, I have come to my own definition of fantasy by way of the tremors that have shaken the science fiction world. Science fiction is no longer called that. The initials SF remain, but the words have undergone a sea change. Such writing has been called alternately science fantasy and speculative fiction.

It seems to me that *speculative fiction* is an excellent definition for fantasy in general. Fantasy is fiction that speculates on the possibilities that this and other worlds hold, limitless possibilities. As the famous mathematician and biologist J. B. S. Haldane says, "How do you know that the planet Mars isn't carried around by an angel?" We don't know—not really. It depends upon the level of reality that we are looking for. It is up to the author of speculative fiction to give us windows that open onto all those possible worlds.

Created worlds

Those possible worlds can be divided into three categories:
Earthbound, Fairie, and *Tourist.*

Earthbound fantasies are stories in which the action takes
place in the world in which we live, though some of the char-
acters may be fantastical. Examples of this kind of story are
The Wind in the Willows (Kenneth Grahame), *James and the
Giant Peach* (Roald Dahl), *Mistress Masham's Repose* (T. H.
White), *The Borrowers* (Mary Norton), *Charlotte's Web*
(E. B. White), *The Bat-Poet* (Randall Jarrell), and *Mary
Poppins* (Pamela Travers). These are all earthbound fanta-
sies, though it is an earth full of wonders we will never meet
outside the pages of the books. These are books that fulfill
Tolkien's request that fantasy be founded "on a recognition
of fact but not a slavery to it."

The second category, *Fairie* is named after the mythic land
where the fairy creatures dwelt. In these books, the action
takes place in a world that is totally apart from ours, that
impinges on our Earth neither in time nor space. (However,
these tales may, in Wallace Stegner's words, be constructed
with "the geography of Hope," that is fantastic worlds made
out of real ones. Much of England, for example, is in Tolkien's
The Lord of the Rings though it is never identified as such.)
Outstanding examples of *Fairie* fantasy, besides *The Hobbit*
and *The Lord of the Rings,* are *The Wizard of Earthsea* and
Tatsinda.

Finally, there are *Tourist* fantasies in which a traveler from
Earth finds his way to another world or into another time and
adventures there. *Alice in Wonderland,* C. S. Lewis' Narnia
books and *The Phantom Tollbooth* by Norton Juster are examples of the best *Tourist* travels to other worlds; *Tom's
Midnight Garden,* by Philippa Pearce and *A Connecticut*

Yankee in King Arthur's Court, by Mark Twain, of travel to other times.

With a little judicious juggling, most literary fantasies will fall readily into one of these categories. Only an occasional brilliant work, like T. H. White's *The Once and Future King,* will cross class lines and succeed.

Beliefs and bugaboos

Fantasy in the guise of myth is as old as language. According to some philosophers, notably Ernst Cassirer, it may even be impossible to have language without myth. Whenever thunder clapped in the ages of prehistoric man, and man grunted his word for thunder, he was at once stating language and the myth of the god-who-thunders. They arose simultaneously. Myth is the shadow-side of language, to paraphrase philologist Max Müller. Myth is the great-grandfather of literary fantasy.

But between prehistoric man's grunting acceptance of the drumming thunder deity, then the well-defined genealogies of the older gods, to the speculation of modern literary fantasies first devised in the seventeenth century French Court, lie many thousands of years of belief.

Belief is still the key word for making fantasy live.

Kenneth Grahame, the author of *The Wind in the Willows,* had this to say about the kind of belief that a reader brings to fantasy: "Whatever its components," he writes of a fantasy story, "truth is not necessarily one of them. A dragon, for instance, is a more enduring animal than a pterodactyl. I have never yet met anyone who really believed in a pterodactyl, but every honest person believes in dragons—down in the back-kitchen of his consciousness."

So we come to the first great rule about writing a fantasy book—belief. But belief works both ways. Not only must the reader believe in the work of fantasy he is reading, the author must believe in it as well.

Belief begets belief. If the writer is skeptical of his own creation, then the reader will be, too. That skepticism on the author's part translates itself into condescension. The book would reek of it. The book would say: "I, of course, don't believe a word of this stuff. But you, dear kiddies, will gobble it up." Condescension is the biggest bugaboo of the children's book world. It bespeaks disbelief, and disbelief is catching. Socrates recognized this unfortunate tendency centuries ago. He said about a writer of myths—of speculative fiction—that "he is not to be envied who has to invent them; much labor and ingenuity will be required of him. . . . and if he is skeptical [of his creation] and would fain reduce them one after another to the rules of probability, this sort of crude philosophy will take up all his time."

The fantasist must believe as he is writing. If it helps to make up genealogical charts as Tolkien did for *The Lord of the Rings,* do it. If it helps to lay out a chess game as Lewis Carroll did for *Through the Looking Glass,* do it. If it helps to close your eyes and talk in the voices of your characters as I do, do it.

You must surrender yourself to your fantasy, if only for the time you are writing it. If you do it for good, then I am afraid you are certifiable. That is the problem when a fantasy world becomes totally real. The person who does not fantasize at all is subhuman, for language and myth make the man. The person who fantasizes all the time and cannot distinguish between fantasy and reality is insane. To surrender yourself to your own fantasy for a certain space of time is not only permissible; it is—in the case of a writer of speculative fiction—imperative. After all, you are asking the reader for more than just Coleridge's "willing suspension of disbelief." You are asking the reader, for the space of the book's pages, to surrender himself totally to your world. As George MacDonald wrote, in his now-classic fantasy tale, *The Golden Key*:

> The Old Man of the Earth stooped over the floor of the cave, raised a huge stone from it, and left it leaning. It disclosed a great hole that went plumb-down.
> "That is the way," he said.
> "But there are no stairs."
> "You must throw yourself in. There is no other way."

That is what the author must ask of the reader: to throw himself into the fantasy. There *is* no other way.

If you call forth the reaction to your work that E. B. White once did from me, you will have succeeded. My father came home one day from work to find my mother and me dissolved in tears. "My God," he shouted, fearing the worst had happened to my baby brother. "What is it, what has happened?" "Oh, Daddy," I cried, "Charlotte is dead." "Charlotte? Charlotte? I don't know any Charlotte," he said puzzled. It took several minutes of misunderstanding before we could make it snufflingly clear that a spider in a book called *Charlotte's Web* had died. We had just been reading it together. My father, though, was quite right. He did not know any Charlotte, for he had never read the book. But my mother and I knew Charlotte. We both knew her well. And we had been with her when she died.

The laws of fantasy

That kind of belief on a reader's part can be brought about only by two things. The first is the writer's own belief, but equally important is the sense of fair play.

By fair play I mean the logic that must be inherent in any fantasy.

May Massee writes: "The right story of fantasy has its feet on the ground."

Lloyd Alexander says: "The Muse in charge of Fantasy wears good sensible shoes."

W. H. Auden warns: ". . . if it is to carry conviction, [the fantasy world must] be a world governed by laws, not by pure chance."

What they are saying is simple, so simple that it has to be considered the one immutable fact of fantasy. The world a writer creates may have as its laws that the inhabitants are nothing but a pack of cards, that animals converse intelligently while messing about in boats, or that a magic ring can make its bearer invisible at the long, slow cost of his soul. But once these laws are set down, the writer cannot, on a whim, set them aside. They must work in the fantasy world as surely as gravity works in ours.

The tools that you use to make the unreal real are three: *place, character, style.*

First, *place.* The piling up of corroborating details helps inspire the reader's belief in a fantastical world. If you read carefully any of the fantasy novels mentioned in this chapter, you will see that the authors have such a visual sense of their fantasy world that it is impossible not to see it through their eyes. In Eleanor Cameron's words, they have a sense of "the compelling power of place."

This is a description from *Alice in Wonderland,* as Alice is falling down the rabbit hole:

> Either the well was very deep, or she fell very slowly, for she had plenty of time as she went down to look about her, and to wonder what was going to happen next. First, she tried to look down and make out what she was coming to, but it was too dark to see anything: then she looked at the sides of the well, and noticed that they were filled with cupboards and book-shelves; here and there she saw maps and pictures hung upon pegs. She took down a jar from one of the shelves as she passed: it was labeled ORANGE MARMALADE, but to her great disappointment it was empty: she did not like to drop the jar, for fear

of killing somebody underneath, so managed to put it into one
of the cupboards as she fell past it.

And this is from the first of the Narnia books (C. S. Lewis),
The Lion, the Witch and the Wardrobe, a description of Mr.
Tumnus' parlor. Mr. Tumnus happens to be a faun, and he
has invited young Lucy to tea:

> Lucy thought she had never been in a nicer place. It was a
> little, dry, clean cave of reddish stone with a carpet on the floor
> and two little chairs ("one for me and one for a friend," said
> Mr. Tumnus) and a table and a dresser and a mantelpiece over
> the fire and above that a picture of an old Faun with a grey beard.
> In one corner there was a door which Lucy thought must lead to
> Mr. Tumnus' bedroom, and on one wall was a shelf full of books.
> Lucy looked at these while he was setting out the tea things. They
> had titles like *The Life and Letters of Silenus* or *Nymphs and
> Their Ways* or *Men, Monks and Gamekeepers: A Study in
> Popular Legend* or *Is Man a Myth?*

And this last is a description of the wizard's warren under
the fountain, from my book, *The Wizard of Washington
Square*:

> The Wizard sat in a large velvet-cushioned oak chair in front
> of a tremendous table. The table was as long as a large door and
> had nine sturdy legs, each ending in a claw. One claw clutched a
> wooden ball and, at odd moments, it would suddenly roll the ball
> to another leg. Then that claw would snatch the ball and stand
> very proudly on it. In this way, every few minutes the table would
> take on a slightly different tilt. Each time the game began again,
> all the beakers and bowls and pitchers and jars on top of the
> table—for the table was littered with glassware and crockery
> —would jangle and clank. But surprisingly, nothing was ever
> broken.

These details of place are precise. The jar of marmalade
from the long, dark tunnel cupboard; the book titles that
would surely be on any genteel faun's bookshelf; the crockery

set a-rattling on the table's surface. Nothing is fuzzy or wishy-washy or only partially visualized. There is no doubt that the authors have been there. They believe. The readers are, therefore, left believing too.

If, as Henry James says about the novel, its supreme virtue is its "solidity of specification," that must be twice as true about a work of fantasy. For in a work of everyday fiction, if you say "apartment" or "ranch house" or "meadow," there are immediate sympathetic vibrations set up in a reader. The reader will know from experience—either direct or indirect—what an apartment or ranch house or meadow looks like. Any description the author gives will be merely secondary information. But if you say "tunnel cupboard" or "faun's parlor" or "wizard's warren," it will mean absolutely nothing to a reader without a verbal visit that includes very specific details.

It all has to be done very solidly, and it has to be very real. Lloyd Alexander, in talking about his own work in the Prydain books, wrote: "What appears gossamer is underneath solid as prestressed concrete."

Perhaps it will help you, before you even begin a fantasy novel, to write out a travelogue of your world. Take yourself for a trip to its most famous points of interest. Or pretend you are writing an article for an encyclopedia that will include customs, laws, historical background, flora and fauna, and the Gross National Product. It will help you develop that "solidity of specification" which James so prized. Even if you never use half the material you have gathered for your mythical land, it will help you construct it for the reader. Remember, too, what you don't put down can be as important as what you do. Lao-Tse in his *Tao Te Ching* wrote that in a vessel of clay, it is the emptiness inside that makes it useful. And Wang Wei, a great Chinese poet-painter, said: "The ultimate concern of the artist is not to paint mountains and clouds and trees but the air between them." So it is, also, with writing.

Character

Just as carefully, the fantasist has to build character. Where a realistic novelist might get away with a sloppy physical description, a hasty pan across the features of a major player, the fantasist must work in careful close-ups. After all, you will often be working with characters who, in addition to their regular personality quirks, have physical quirks as well. Not many of us have met one of E. Nesbit's Psammeads or a Hobbit or a Puddleglum on our daily rounds, nor can we summon one up in our mind's eye unless we have already read the proper book. Even if we have met a lion or an English nanny or a stuffed bear here on Earth, they are not anything like Aslan or Mary Poppins or Winnie-the-Pooh. Once you have met *them*, the whole of lionhood and English nannyhood and stuffed animalhood are transformed. In Tolkien's words, "By the making of Pegasus, horses were enobled." And we, too, are transformed, just by that meeting.

Again, the magic that works the transformation is the magic of detail. The piling up of visual attributes is what, in the end, utterly convinces. Often some marvelously homely detail puts the cap on the character and transforms the utterly unreal into something real. For example, once you know that E. Nesbit's Psammead suffers horribly if he gets wet, you are given a handle to him. And it helps to know that Hobbits are homebodies who love a good smoke, a pint of beer, and spin long and unbroken tales about their family trees. How can these characters not be real when you know these intimate details about them?

It is important, too, to spell out the horrors, to describe vividly the wicked villains. They should not be shrugged off the way early horror story writers like H. P. Lovecraft used to shrug off their great gloppy things that went bump in the night. They used sentences such as, "It was the ineffable" and "It was the unknowable" and "It was the inutterable." Modern young readers do not suffer from Victorian sensibilities where horror is concerned. And the best of the fantasy tales makes a horror utterable and knowable and effable. They categorize the horrors with as much detail as they can muster. Or stomach.

After the close-ups of a mythical creature's physical quirks, a fantasy writer then must deal with the creature's character quirks as well. Once you have described a great fanged villain, you are not done with him. He must also have a believable character to go with his twitches—inner twitches to match the outer ones. In that way, the fantasy writer has much the same problem as any other novelist. The characters must live through both dialogue and action. No small problem, of course, but not unique to fantasy.

Style

What is unique to fantasy is the role played by style.

Most fantasies, and especially what is known as High Fantasy—where the battles of good and evil are played out on a new and magical landscape—are written in a style that is akin to poetry. It is also a style of writing that recalls the great hero tales and the legends of our past, when bards sang their stories and did not just tell them.

Critics of this poetic style have labeled it "mock heroic" or "mock epic." But when it is done correctly, the poetic style is perfect for the telling of a fantasy tale.

Camus has written: "You tell me of an invisible planetary system in which electrons gravitate around a nucleus. You explain this world to me with an image. I realize then that you have been reduced to poetry." He sees that when we describe what goes on in the *real* world of the atom, we are, in his curious phrase, "reduced to poetry." So, too, when we fully describe a new world, a new system, where different immutable laws reign, we must create them in the language of poetry.

"In the beginning God created the heavens and the earth." *That* is poetry. And the fantasy writer must not strive for less in his creation.

It is hardly surprising, therefore, that many of the best fantasy novels have been written by poets. And very few books of fantasy are without some kind of poems, whether in the guise of songs or spells or incantations or the naming of names. Oscar Wilde, Walter de la Mare, Carl Sandburg, Randall Jarrell are all poets. They also have each written beautiful fantasy tales.

The poetic instinct is only one form that the love of words takes on. Word play is another. Word play is especially abundant in humorous fantasy tales. Nonsense—which is turning words inside out—and punning are two kinds of word play that are often found in fantasy.

Remember the Mock Turtle talking about the schools of fish who learn their two R's—"reeling and writhing"—and of the old turtle teacher who was called a Tortoise, even though he wasn't one, because "he taught us." Remember *The Phantom Tollbooth*'s Kingdom of Dictionopolis, ruled by King Azaz the Unabridged, that lay right next to the land called The Doldrums. Remember Roald Dahl's *Charlie and the Chocolate Factory*'s storeroom #77 that contained "All the beans, CACAO BEANS, COFFEE BEANS, JELLY BEANS, and HAS BEANS," and my own book, *Commander Toad in Space,* in which the brave and bright toad commands the ship "Star Warts" and overcomes the sea monster Deep Wader.

Poets and fantasists have this in common—a love and respect for all aspects of the language. Fantasists and bards have this in common—what they compose can be sung.

Vision

It is not only in style that fantasy is close to the old bardic tales, but in vision also. There is an epic sweep in the best fantasy, a chance to play out the large gestures, the eternal passions, the battles of good and evil that each of us meets daily on a small scale.

While realistic fiction deals with small truths, fantasy by its very remove from reality can deal with Truth with a capital T. Realistic fiction shows us the tiny evasions and lies we all indulge in every day. Fantasy shows us the Great Lie. If as Alfred North Whitehead says: "Literature only exists to express and develop that imaginative world which is our life, the kingdom which is within us," then fantasy shows us the widest borders of that kingdom and sounds the depths of that world.

It is this imaginative probing, the expressing of primitive fears, that makes some adults mistrust fantasy as unhealthy. I have many times heard the argument that books of fantasy wean the child from the real world, give him no hold on reality. In an article in *Publishers Weekly* about realistic books, author Julius Lester put this argument into a passionate statement when he wrote: "In a world in which a child can be dead of an overdose of heroin at age twelve, Snow White is not only inadequate, it is in danger of being vulgar."

But Lester himself told me that he made such a sweeping statement to get people to examine and question fantasy's validity. I did—and I disagree with his statement. Snow

White might not make direct contact with the world of a child who has very real problems of drugs, racism, poverty. Still, I do not think that Snow White—or any fantasy or folk tale—is totally irrelevant, inadequate, verging on the vulgar. It is another door, another opening, another kind of experience. The world of the subconscious is a very *real* world, and ofttimes these books speak more directly to a child than a realistic one. As Wallace Hildeck has written in *Children and Fiction*: "By taking us into another world [books] can widen our experience, and widening our experience, [books] can help cultivate our sympathies, giving them depth and extending their range."

Whimsy or fantasy, stories of the unreal, speculative fiction hone an aesthetic appreciation in the young reader, teaching him about other things that can be found in life, in art, in the realm of the imagination.

However, this distrust for the efficacy of fantasy books sometimes extends to the editors, too. Despite sales reports to the contrary, they find fantasy "hard to sell" and often cannot read with an open mind the fantasy books submitted to them.

Even such a book as Madeleine L'Engle's Newbery-winning *A Wrinkle in Time* was rejected by almost thirty editors until it found a sympathetic ear and eye at Farrar, Straus.

The fantasy novel often, in its imaginative probing, is too much to bear.

The fact is that the best fantasy, by its very power to move the reader, by its dramatic—even melodramatic—morality finally does something else. It instills values.

Not that these books should set out to moralize. That would indeed be, as the Queen of Hearts says, "Sentence first, verdict afterwards." But one can moralize without setting a moral. As the Master Hand in Ursula K. Le Guin's

The Wizard of Earthsea says to Ged, the young apprentice magician, "To light a candle is to cast a shadow."

The writer lights many candles in a good fantasy novel. The shadows they cast in a child's soul will last for the rest of his life.

*The need to know surely and accurately is a
basic hunger. . . .*

—May Hill Arbuthnot

6

Creative Nonfiction

"Now WHAT I want is facts. Teach these boys and girls
nothing but Facts. Facts alone are wanted in life. Plant
nothing else and root out everything else. You can form the
minds of reasoning animals only upon facts. Nothing else will
ever be of any service to them."

Does that sound like your ninth-grade teacher? Or a local
librarian? Or the principal of your child's elementary school?
It is actually Mr. Gradgrind in Dickens' *Hard Times*. Yet
over a hundred years later, there are still educators who
echo the sentiments of the unsentimental Mr. G.

I even met an eight-year-old boy who sounded like him.
He cornered me one day after having dismissed my gift to
him of a fantasy book with a contemptuous sniff.

"You know what boys my age like?" he inquired rhe-
torically. "They like *real* books. They like the facts."

To my eight-year-old friend, *real* was equivalent to *facts*.

"Just the facts, ma'am," as Sgt. Joe Friday used to say on a TV show. It was useless for me to try to quote my young friend William Blake's letter of 1799: "You certainly Mistake, when you say that the Visions of Fancy are not to be found in This World. To me This World is all One continued Vision of Fancy or Imagination." My eight-year-old was mistaking raw facts for information. And it is information, not just raw facts that most children want.

Information or facts

It is important to draw that distinction immediately when talking about nonfiction: facts, or data, *vs.* information, or what the data says.

For example, if a boatman stands at the bow and shouts: "Mark twelve, mark ten, mark six, mark four, mark twain," he is giving data to the helmsman. But the helmsman is receiving the following information: "The water is getting awfully shallow. Do something, quick."

An untrained ear would not hear the information, only the facts.

It is the nonfiction writer's problem to turn that data into information. Data is useful only to the trained ear and eye. As information it speaks to anyone who takes the time to listen. Information is useful, it is palatable, it is fascinating. And it is compelling to the reader.

Changing data into information is a creative process. It is the first of a series of processes that make the writing of nonfiction as creative as the writing of fiction.

Changing data into information consists of organizing, distilling, and processing. It consists of making comparisons and finding commonalities. All these things can be summed up in one word: *recognition*.

For example, I wrote a book about the history and lore of

kite flying, *World on a String.* At first I had an assortment of facts: kites began almost 3000 years ago in China; religious kite flying is done in Japan; intricate centipede and dragon kites abound in Korea; weather kites were important in America; Marconi used a kite antenna for his wireless experiments; Benjamin Franklin flew a kite in a thunderstorm and proved the sky was full of electricity. Lots of data. But then I began to see a common thread, a theme—kites rose in the East and flowered there in beauty and serenity. When they traveled to the West, they became useful. And *that* is information. Once I had that, the book began to achieve a balance, a point of view, a style, and all because I had found a thread that could wind through the narrative of my kite history.

Or another example from my own writing: I was working on a biography of George Fox, the first Quaker. I had a lot of facts, data. Fox was arrested for refusing to sign an oath of loyalty to the king; he was put in jail for refusing to fight in the Commonwealth army; he was beaten by mobs for preaching that God lives in every man. Then I began to see that George Fox had a lot to say to the young people of today. With his long hair and funny clothes, with his pronouncements in favor of women, against slavery, against war—even with his funny "thee's" and "thou's"—he had a spirit that matched any of the young radicals of our era. He was a man who, in modern terminology, was not afraid to put his body on the line. Again—information—a thread that could run through the entire book.

What I achieved in those two books is what Arthur Koestler speaks of in *The Act of Creation.* He calls it "The sudden shaking together of two previously unconnected matrices." It is known as the Eureka Act in science. It is known as the *A-ha* in Gestalt Therapy. It is the light bulb above a person's head in the comic strips. It is *recognition.*

Creative research

Another creative part of nonfiction is the research for a book on a factual subject. Research *can* be only a collecting of data. It can be the journalist's who-what-when-where-how. But the truly creative researcher is the one who asks not only what happened, but *what does it mean?* Not only how did it happen, but *how does it affect other things?* In other words, the creative researcher is thinking of data to the nth degree, data raised to the plane of information. The creative researcher is actively seeking out ways of turning data—at the very moment of researching—into information. When you do this, you are going to find more data because you are going to be moving on several planes at once.

Creative research is made up of four parts: intuitive guesses, detective work, *chutzpah,* and just plain luck. The first three you can cultivate. The last, somehow, always follows after, like the tail on one of Bo-Peep's sheep.

The *intuitive guess* is the competent, educated guess which leads a researcher on to discovery. It is what Suzanne Langer meant when she wrote that "Most discoveries are suddenly seen things that were always there."

The *detective work* is the initial background stage, the finding of various sources. Here are some books which can short-cut your detective work: *Reference Books: A Brief Guide,* published by the Enoch Pratt Free Library, 400 Cathedral Street, Baltimore, Maryland 21201, for your home shelf. Any good library will have a more detailed list of reference books in the *Guide to Reference Books,* by Constance Winchell. Checking the *Reader's Guide to Periodical Literature* will tell you about magazine articles on your subject in over 150 different periodicals. *The American Library Directory* and the *Subject Collection: A Guide to Special*

Book Collections in Libraries are also helpful. *Poole's Index to Periodical Literature* lists the contents of American and British magazines published between 1802 and 1906. *The New York Times Index* has bound volumes and a microfilm index that go back to 1851. And *The London Times Index* goes all the way back to 1790. *The Cumulative Book Index* has a history from 1898. These help you to zero in on the available material. Once you have done the necessary detective work, you are ready to begin.

Chutzpah, the Yiddish word for gall or guts, is what you need in tracking down another source of background material —individuals who can help you. Since researching in books alone often leaves you with a dry, stolid view of a subject, it helps to find someone with a connection to your subject who can give you a new view. Contacting such a person—or persons—often takes guts, gall, *chutzpah*.

And your just plain *luck* will follow after.

Let me give you an example of how this four-part backgrounding works. When I was a child I devoured pirate books. For some reason known only to my ten-year-old self, I had a collective crush on Captain Kidd, Henry Morgan, and Blackbeard. In the course of my reading, well before the women's liberation movement drew a new breath, I happened upon two women pirates—Anne Bonney and Mary Reade. Years later, thinking of a subject for a nonfiction book, I remembered these two "ladies."

It was then I made my *intuitive guess:* where there were two women pirates, there were probably more. Rarely is such a thing a completely isolated phenomenon. I had heard of women like Deborah Sampson disguising themselves as men and joining the Revolutionary army. Why not women doing the same aboard ship? Surely, I told myself, there are more than two female pirates. It turned out that I was correct.

Then I began my detective work. One magazine I tracked

down was a one-shot entitled *Treasure Hunters*. The author, Robert I. Nesmith, had a minuscule biography opposite the contents page, which mentioned that he lived in Rye, New York. So I turned my *detective work* into *chutzpah*.

Rye, New York was one town away from my parents' home. I made a point of calling Mr. Nesmith the next time I visited my mother and father. I was ready to invite myself over to talk about pirates—and ladies—with him.

And that was when *luck* came in, wagging behind. Mr. Nesmith invited me over immediately. He turned out to have the world's largest collection of published and unpublished piratania. He was so delighted with my novel idea, that he not only gave me free run of his library and helped me research, but his wife baked fresh cookies for each session as well. *Luck,* indeed. *Pirates in Petticoats* was published in 1963, and it is still the only book of its kind around.

Notes and files

So you begin amassing your data. Some writers put their notes in little notebooks or large looseleafs; some on scraps of paper. I believe, however, that the best way is the traditional filing system. File cards are easily arranged and re-arranged as your book grows, they are easy to carry into libraries, and any stationery store can restock them if you run out.

Take care. Notes taken one, two, three months ago in haste might as well have been taken by a Martian as yourself. Here is some necessary advice:

1. Write clearly and precisely in pen.

2. Put in quotes *anything* that comes directly from a source and scribble "paraphrase" or "mine" next to anything that is your own interpretation. Charges of plagiarism—whether conscious or unconscious copying—can ruin a writer forever.

3. Note on each card the name of the book, author, and the library where you found it. If you are using a number of different libraries, you can waste many precious hours trying to trace a book just to check a quote if you do not remember where you found the book.

4. Check each book's bibliography and write *its* sources down. In that way, you enlarge the scope of your own research.

These may sound like simple-minded rules, but I have written seven nonfiction books and have found these things out in the most painful way—by experience.

Once you have amassed your data, thought about some connecting links, and made your initial *A-ha's*, you are ready to write your nonfiction book.

The writing phase: outlines

Jean Karl, the juvenile editor at Atheneum, asks this question in her *From Childhood to Childhood*: ". . . how will authors demonstrate where facts imbedded in wisdom can lead? How can authors create books that will make children yearn for wisdom that lies beyond facts, without preaching, without pouring either the facts or the children into precast molds?"

Those are questions worth pondering before and during your writing phase. The problem is to put the meat (information) on the bones (data) without preaching. To teach without sounding as though you are teaching, reaching out not only for new subjects but for new approaches.

The new approach begins, of course, when you make your first *A-ha*. It continues through the next step—making an outline.

Outlines are an absolute necessity when writing nonfiction. An outline is like a road map. Whether the territory is previously explored or not, a road map will let you see at a glance the entire area to be traveled. It will also help you when the going gets rough. But just as road maps are updated whenever new roads have been added, so an outline has to change as the data and information grow. When the writer really gets into his information, when he experiences the Eureka phenomenon, it is inevitable (and exciting, too) that the outline will have to be changed. An outline must be a road map, but it is also like the skin of a snake which the snake sheds annually in order to accommodate a fuller form.

The outline can serve another function, too. It is a selling tool. If your subject is strange enough, original enough, then you may be able to tease an editor into a contract with the outline alone. I did this with *Pirates in Petticoats* and each of my subsequent nonfiction books: *World on a String, Friend: the Story of George Fox and the Quakers, The Wizard Islands, Ring Out: A Book of Bells, Simple Gifts: The Story of the Shakers,* and *Touch Magic.* The outlines were not trivial matters, but detailed chapter-by-chapter plans of the books. In the case of *Friend* and *The Wizard Islands* and this book, the outline was also accompanied by prefatory material, author's notes, and forewords. Some of my outlines have been as long as twenty pages. In each instance, the final book was quite different from the original outline—better, I think, because I had additional information by the time I had finished.

An example of my own outline technique follows. It is from a seven-page outline that I submitted for my biography *Friend: The Story of George Fox and the Quakers.*

George Fox and the Inner Light
OUTLINE

Ch. 1: The Righteous Christer
"If George says Verily, there is no altering him."
Birth and early life of George Fox, growing up in a poor but religious English home in the seventeenth century.

Physical description and a character sketch of Fox. Also a sketch of the religious temper of the mid-seventeenth century that culminated in the great achievements of religious toleration and constitutional monarchy. It stemmed mainly from the upsurge of *personal* religion among the common people.

Ch. 2: The Man in Leather Breeches
"Here are my leather breeches which frighten all the priests and professors."
Early preaching and brutal jail experiences of Fox. His growth as a mystic, a proselytizer, and a strong man of religion who set himself up against the established churches with their priests and the wandering preachers of some 176 different sects. Fox's attack on organized religion, the priesthood, the churches as "houses" of God. His use of plain speech. His early convictions of the brotherhood of men, God in every man, and his jailings for these convictions.

I included a thumbnail sketch of Fox's life in two pages, five pages of chapter-by-chapter breakdown, and a five-page prologue that was eventually used, almost word-for-word, in the book. But the above two chapter descriptions became chapters 1–5 in the finished book, for, as my knowledge of George Fox grew, so did the book. And what began as a projected ten-chapter biography ended up seventeen long chapters, plus a prologue and an epilogue, and an Author's Note to boot.

Good books grow. Good outlines allow such growth.

There are basically four kinds of nonfiction books for young readers: biography, history, science, and how-to. Occasionally they overlap one another. Each has problems peculiar to its genre, but they all have several things in common.

The primary danger facing anyone writing a nonfiction book for young readers is style. You must sail between the Scylla and Charybdis of jargon and cuteness.

On the one hand, there is the danger of falling back on the jargon of your field. Especially in the sciences and social sciences this is true. But it also happens in how-to books. Aldous Huxley, in a brilliant though dense book, *Literature and Science,* roundly castigates the scientists for their self-imposed jabberwocky. He jibes: "A rose is a rose is a rose is RNA, DNA, polypeptide chares of amino acids. . . ." But at the same time he takes a swipe at the poets and "creative" writers who are afraid to tackle scientific subjects. Why shouldn't we have a Norman Mailer's *Of a Fire on the Moon* for children? Or James Watson's *The Double Helix* for budding young scientists?

If jargon is the danger on the one hand, an equal danger is coyness. Many writers affect it when writing for young people. It is the little-books-for-little-minds syndrome. However, it possible to write creative nonfiction without falling back into soppy storylines or the dear-reader's style that is so condescending.

In a *New York Times Book Review* article, Eve Merriam satirized this horrible tendency with a piece entitled "The Poolitzer Prizes." She made up titles like *Let's Find Out about Doughnut Holes, Hortense the Happy Hypotenuse* and *Our Friend the Battery Cell.* What makes these titles so very devastating is that they are perilously close to titles editors reject—or publish—daily.

Making data come alive

A ridiculous storyline is not necessary in order to capture a child's interest in a nonfiction idea. But something *is* needed to make the data come alive to a child reader. Since data alone —"Just the facts, ma'am"—cannot give the young reader an adequate handle on a factual subject, the writer must supply a substitute handle. Again, that is where the creative part of creative nonfiction comes in.

An interesting and devastating comment on the state of nonfiction comes from a literary agent of my acquaintance. She writes, "The more intellectual nonfiction books are not going so well these days. The more mass-market books, books that *entertain,* are in demand." In place of serious, well-reasoned and deep books on issues and historical happenings, on famous people and famous events, the how-to, puzzle-and-magic, and craft books are selling well. There is a compromise position authors of nonfiction can take—between the dry, pedantic and the entertaining. That compromise is another province of creativity.

At the end of any book of nonfiction, for whatever age group it is intended, you should append two things—an index and a bibliography. It will be up to the editor to decide if the book actually needs a very detailed bibliography. Perhaps a simple "Recommended for Further Reading" list will do. However, you should send it along for two reasons: It authenticates your material, and it gives the copy editor a leg up on checking and rechecking your facts and quotes. Every author, even the best and most precise scholar, makes an occasional mistake in copying or typing. That is one of the reasons a publishing house has a copy editor—to catch any little mistake. The index cannot, of course, be handled until the book is in page proofs, since page references are needed. Often the publisher will hire a professional indexer to make your index for you, but many authors prefer to do their own.

Biography

Elizabeth Gray Vining, a novelist of note, has written that one day the figure of William Penn came up and tapped her on the shoulder. After that, she had to write his biography.

All biographies should be written that way—when an historical personage taps you on the shoulder. You do not have to love or admire the person. You do not even have to like him. But you need to empathize with your subject. And when you are tapped on the shoulder, you should respond.

When I wrote the biography *Friend,* I was tapped in just that way by the fiery mystic George Fox. After spending more than a year with Fox, walking the length and breadth of seventeenth-century England with him, I became a member of the Religious Society of Friends.

I am not suggesting that any biographer of Lao-Tse become a Taoist or an author who writes about the Marquis de Sade become a practicing sadist. What I am saying is that when you are writing a biography, you should make a strong commitment to your subject.

Such a commitment does not preclude objectivity. Indeed, especially in biography, the writer must be prepared to see the other side of the historical coin. A biographer must not sell his soul, as one wit put it, "for a pot of message."

The biographer has to be able to be both committed and objective. There is not one saint or sinner whose life story would not be more readable, more recognizable, more affecting if the objective truths were sifted from the subjective myths. As George Sims cynically puts it, "All biographies should have the subtitle: myth versus reality." Keep his suggestion in mind as you write, so that you will *not* have to append such a subtitle.

Especially in writing the lives of saints, one has to walk carefully between worship and cynical disdain, between hagiography and "debunkum." Nothing is duller to the reader than a series of incidents in the life of a "totally virtuous" man or woman. But if you scratch the surface of most of the so-called "totally virtuous" saints, you will find them human. It is their very humanity rather than their godliness that makes them so fascinating. St. Paul without sin—uninteresting. Dr. Donne without the libertine John—unthinkable. Ghandi without his early marriage problems—dehumanized. What makes these people "saints" is the fact that they rose above their human problems. What makes others "sinners" is that they sank under the weight.

I found it so with George Fox. He was a man who was all but canonized by his followers. (Probably only the fact that Quakers did not believe in the sainthood of a man or woman saved him.) Because injudicious editing by a succession of believer-secretaries had all but taken the country boy and man out of his *Journal,* Fox was long a mystical enigma to both his followers and detractors. A powerful speaker, his words became dull when committed to paper and purified by his loving help. To hear the real Friend George, I read his epistles and speeches out loud. I even read some of them outdoors, where much of Fox's preaching had convinced early Quakers.

If Fox's loving followers had all but submerged his electric personality with their censorship, his detractors were even worse. To listen to contemporary name-callers, many of them men of substance and learning, Fox's power was not his own but of the devil's making. They called him a witch, a magician, a pervert, a womanizer, a madman, a liar, and the anti-Christ. To the learned priests, he was a honey-tongued farm boy bent on subverting the church's superstructure. To the rich landowners and minor nobility, he was an upstart preacher trying to change society's strata. To the man on the street, he was a crowd-pleaser who touted the equality of such subhumans as blacks, Indians, and women.

To write about such a man—indeed to write *any* biography —one must balance both positions: sinner and saint. How to find the man or woman behind the mask of history is the problem. That is the challenge, of course, cutting through history's tidyings-up, sorting through the legends that all powerful persons leave in their wakes.

It is important in writing biographies to get to the source. The scholars call the material that issued either directly from the mouth or pen of the subject or from contemporaries *primary sources*. *Secondary sources* are all that has been written since.

Quotations

Which brings us to the biggest technical problem in writing biography: to quote or not to quote.

There are two schools of thought on the problem of quotations. The first holds that you can put into quotes only what has been documented, either in direct speech or conversations reported by friends, letters from the subject or journals. André Maurois outlined this orthodox view succinctly: "Under no account has the biographer a right to invent a single fact. . . . He should not put into his hero's mouth nor attribute to any character, sentences they have not spoken." I would add to that, *or written*.

The second school holds that you can make an approximation of what the subject probably would have said in such circumstances, using things the subject has said or written in similar situations or simply making an educated guess based on thorough period research. Margery Fisher explains this view in her excellent book, *Matters of Fact*: "To draw a line too sharply between known fact and reasonable deduction would be to deny (children) a great deal of persuasive detail."

I myself am a practitioner of the more orthodox view, though my first book, *Pirates in Petticoats,* is replete with imagined conversations. I now feel that, if it is biography, what you quote from your subject's mouth must be documentable. Interpolated conversations belong to historical fiction. If you write such a book, a "story biography," as Margery Fisher calls it, be sure that words to the effect that "A novel based on the life of _____" are under your title.

The main problem facing a biographer is that he must make sense out of a subject, he must go beyond actions to interpret character. In fact, there must be a good deal of the lay psychologist and the novelist in every biographer. Margery Fisher puts it this way: "Biography is an illusion, a fiction in the guise of fact." It is an especially exciting kind of book to write—precisely because of these problems.

History

When writing a book about history, it is important to remember that no historical period or historical event exists in a vacuum. Once not so long ago—about twenty years to be exact—history in the schools was taught as a succession of certain names, dates, places. I know, for I was taught that way. But today, the emphasis is on *understanding* what led to those certain names, dates, places.

So the writer of nonfiction books of history must guide the young reader into making the connections between past and present, or between the past and present of that book. The emphasis is on that word "guide." For children are not, as Jean Karl warns, "small vessels crying to be filled with the word of truth, but rational individuals who can think for themselves."

The research for an historical book may lead you into many unsuspected backwaters. Looking up my material for *Friend* introduced me to several characters I would love to put into a novel, incidents that could climax a stirring historical tale, even phrases that suggest a picture book. Nothing is lost in your research. It just gets stored in your files or your memory for further use.

The author of a nonfiction book must remember this simple rule: A steady development of events or facts makes for a steady reader. If you allow yourself many digressions or detours or irrelevancies, your book will be too complex for even the most sophisticated reader. Like a good mystery book, the good historical nonfiction book unfolds its clues.

Some excellent historical books to use as examples are: *To Be a Slave,* by Julius Lester; *Man and Magic,* by Benjamin Appel; *The First Book of American History,* by Henry Steele Commager; *The Story of Mankind,* by Hendrik Van Loon; *Hudson* (Rivers of America Series), by Carl Carmer.

Some excellent biographies for young readers are: *America's Robert E. Lee,* by Henry Steele Commager; *Abraham Lincoln,* by Ingri and Edgar Parin d'Aulaire; *Penn,* by Elizabeth Janet Gray (Elizabeth Gray Vining); *Why Don't You Get a Horse, Sam Adams?* by Jean Fritz.

Science

Popular science for children is fast becoming a new art form. In it, the writer must blend the textbook with reportage, the philosophical essay and a sociological forecast, to paraphrase Huxley.

Unfortunately, there has grown up in the years since science has taken its benevolent toll on man, a feeling that fact and fancy should not mix. Keats damned the man who explained the rainbow, saying he had robbed it of its poetry. Yet, it need not be so. Science fiction is one voice crying this out. And good science writing for children is another.

There are three interesting, poetic, yet scientifically correct methods of blending science and poetry in a book for young

readers, three "tricks of the trade." They are the use of nonverbal or experimental examples, metaphor, and aphorism.

Nonverbal or experimental examples are pictures or experiments that directly involve action on the part of the
reader. They can be as direct as instructions for actual
laboratory experiments. They can be as indirect as one I recall
reading in a picture book about the moon and its relationship
to earth. One child was told to hold a rubber ball, standing
for the moon; another, a beach ball representing the earth;
and the third, a lighted lamp, the sun. As the rubber ball
child and the beach ball child spin around, circling the lamp
child, the beach ball experiences a kind of day and night.
What could be more memorable for the child, more illumi-
nating?

Metaphor is especially apt for scientific books. Metaphor
is, after all, what science is all about. Mathematical formulae,
physical models of biochemical structures—these are really
metaphors for something we cannot see. Again, as Camus
said about the atomic structure, "You explain this world to
me with an image. . . ." It is more easily understood that
way. It is explaining the unfamiliar in terms of the familiar.
For example, in a book my husband is working on, *Computers,
Machines to Reckon With,* he explains that a computer's
register is a pocket for holding numbers. He also explains
that a computer program is a recipe that the computer can
follow. Children who are not familiar with registers and pro-
grams are familiar with pockets and recipes, so both metaphors are easily understood and are very precise. That is
something to remember if you are using metaphor: It must
be exactly appropriate. If it is not, you will have given your
young reader a lie he or she will always remember.

Another way of dealing with information in science books
is by using the aphorism. An aphorism is a short, pithy sen-

tence or sentences that embody the truth. An aphorism is especially useful in writing about technical things for nontechnical readers. It sets the readers into a mode of thought, makes them aware of the author's intentions. For example, when my husband ends the first section of his book this way: "Two things should be kept firmly in mind when you read this book. One—everything is simpler than it seems, especially computers. Two—nothing is as simple as it seems—especially computers," the readers already have an insight into his thinking, and it helps them settle into the rest of the book.

As the approach to history books for children has changed, so too the approach to scientific books for young readers has been overhauled. No longer do books say simply, "This is Truth. Learn it." The emphasis now is on showing, not telling. The child reader is given examples, ideas, and left to draw many of his own conclusions.

How-to books

Finally, the how-to books have captured an ever-growing audience of children. Certain publishing companies deal almost exclusively with these kinds of craft or cooking or make-and-do books; others publish an outstanding one occasionally; still other companies would not be interested in this kind of book at all. A writer interested in doing a book on a how-to subject needs to research the marketability with care. Check catalogues and library shelves. Know the publishing companies who are most keenly interested and send out query letters before actually starting on such a venture. (See Chapter 10 for query letters.)

The keynotes to success in a how-to book are *simplicity, clarity,* and *precision.*

You yourself must be the guinea pig for all your instructions. You must write down exactly what you do step by step. Then you must turn about and try to follow your own instructions to the letter. Writing simple but precise instructions for what is to you the easiest task in the world, is one of the most difficult things to do. I remember working on a series of make-and-do softcover books at a publishing company I worked for. The thing that took most of our editorial time was the checking and rechecking of the directions for crafts and magic tricks. A simple half-twist in a string, an easy knot, a quick holding down of a piece of paper with a pinkie that one does without thinking about it—all these have to be explained ever so precisely to the novice. It is frustrating to detail each step, especially steps one considers common sense. But remember, in any craft what is common sense for one person may be nonsense to another.

It seems to me, on the whole, that there are three things to remember about nonfiction: commitment, style and the second coming, though they are rarely things that nonfiction writers mention. Yet they elevate nonfiction into the truly creative, into literature.

The very fact that we call it *non*fiction does a disservice to the genre. That puts these books in a race with fiction, indicating that they are *already* losers. Yet some of the most beautifully written informational books have changed lives, as surely as fiction has: *The Double Helix, Silent Spring, The Diary of Anne Frank, The Outermost House, King Solomon's Ring, The Hero of a Thousand Faces*—to name some special favorites of mine.

One thing these books have in common—besides the fact that they are informational in the broadest sense—is that their authors wrote them out of the deepest commitment. Not all books that impart information *have* to be written with that kind of passion, but surely a kind of fascination or a deep desire to learn more about a subject *must* be there from the start. Any slackening of interest, any boredom on the author's part will show through at once.

Style is, of course, the particular way of setting down the information gathered. It is taking the many threads and weaving a tapestry. Threads can be forgotten or overlooked. A tapestry is forever. The words in an informational book can sing, can paint pictures, can be infused with a life that draws the reader in, not just the who-what-where-when-how of journalism.

For example, why say prosaically "People are so different, that any stories told about them sound like fairy tales" when you could write—as Georgess McHargue does in *The Impossible People*—"If there have been men who lived in caves and forests, grass huts and stone palaces, why not men who live in the air and under the sea?" And she draws you into her book. In Ann Warren Turner's *Houses for the Dead* and *Rituals of Birth,* two amazing books about two vastly different subjects, she uses her remarkable storytelling ability to focus on the story of a man or woman or child in a life/ death situation that is sociologically and anthropologically correct but are stories first and foremost. The dry facts are given flesh and in that way have the power to move the reader enormously. She succeeds because of style.

The most intriguing thing for me about informational books, however, is the fact of the second coming. Nothing researched is ever lost. Having spent days, weeks, months, even years inside a particular subject, it would be a shame, would it not, to get just *one* book or story out of it? What a waste of time, energy, talent, insight and knowledge. What to do? Recycle. Use it again.

You may not be able, by the terms of your contract, to write another book on *exactly* the same subject. But then— why would you want to? However you can find a different approach, a different angle, a different use of the same material. Let me give you some examples: *Pirates in Petti- coats* led directly to *The Wizard Islands,* a book about ghost and mystery stories on islands. Why? Pirates bury treasure on islands and along the way I had stumbled on several of those tales. Working on my father's book, *A Young Sports- man's Guide to Kite Flying* pushed me into writing my own book about kites, *World On A String.* The stories in the research introduced me to the emperor who became the key character in *The Emperor and the Kite* and the kite bearer who became *The Seventh Mandarin,* both picture story- books. And I found the Shakers so fascinating when I did my research and writing in *Simple Gifts* that I wrote an historical novel, *The Gift of Sarah Barker,* a Romeo and Juliet story set in a Shaker community I called New Vale.

Second coming, indeed.

This final word about nonfiction books is a cautionary one. As we saw in the beginning of this chapter and must be reminded of again in the end, "just the facts, ma'am" is not enough. The importance of nonfiction trade books for children of the twentieth century cannot be too heavily underscored. It is not only that children are little sponges absorbing every bit of specific information that comes their way. It is also, in Huxley's words, that "every concrete particular, public or private, is a window opening onto the universal."

We must give the children we are writing for not only data—the particular—but also a little boost into the universal —with information.

The realities of childhood put to shame the
half-true notions in some children's books.
                              —Maurice Sendak

7

It's Not All Peter Rabbit

A DEAR friend of mine once gave me a pin with Peter Rabbit
on it as a token of my involvement with children's books. It
was a beautiful gesture on her part, but it also symbolized for
me most adults' acquaintance with the field—amused, even
tolerant, interest, bemused acceptance, but a real lack of understanding of the length and breadth of children's literature.

After all, it is not all Peter Rabbit.

Children's books are not all about the fey, about fairies and
elves and talking animals with the kind of coyness that made
Dorothy Parker in her *New Yorker* column "Constant
Reader" dismiss a children's classic with the terse: "Tonstant
weader fwowed up."

Children's books also embrace realism. Not the pseudo-
realism of the Hardy Boys or Tom Swift, the Bobbsey Twins
and Nancy Drew. But nitty-gritty, raw, down-to-the-bone
realism.

The new realism

Don't get mired in that deepest kind of quicksand, belief in the *taboo*. There are no longer any taboos in children's books, except that of good taste. (And depending upon your taste, you might say that even that has fallen by the wayside.) What was once not even whispered in the parlor, and only snickered at in the barroom, is now legitimate fare for young readers.

The old-fashioned view that certain things should be taboo for children simply because they are young is no longer in style. Librarians, who are often caricatured as conservative, accept this, too. (Though occasionally there are librarians whose overzealous guardianship of the "morals of minors" make their sister and brother librarians blanch. For example, in 1972, the American Library Association was in an uproar when some misguided librarians painted diapers on the little naked boy-child in Maurice Sendak's prize-winning picture book, *In the Night Kitchen.*)

The reasons for this opening-up of subject matter in children's books are many and varied. I think that three factors have been most instrumental in bringing about this new phase: the change in readership, the rise of mass media, and especially the advent of television.

Certainly the reading public has changed. Children who were once-upon-a-time chained to long days in a factory are being compulsorily and compulsively "educated." Reading is no longer the royal prerogative of the privileged upper classes. Children at all levels of society are opening books—and opening worlds.

The superabundance of brightly-colored magazines in every household also has a lot to do with the striking down of the taboos. Easily accessible to the youngest children, these periodicals talk about drugs, death, and divorce in the same alluring fashion with which they tout beauty lotions and beer.

And finally television, perhaps the real reason that so much has changed in the last twenty years in children's books. Television with its instant replays of war in the Middle East, terrorist attacks and assassinations of political figures, demonstrations in the major cities of the world, natural disasters, space fantasies, the explicit sexuality in television drama. Even a child who does not yet read is exposed to all of these impressions on TV.

So all the deadly sins, plus sex, death, drugs, drunkenness, divorce, poverty, hunger have all become the subjects of children's books. *Sounder* (William H. Armstrong) looks at white man's brutality to blacks; *My Darling, My Hamburger* (Paul Zindel), at premarital sex, pregnancy and abortion; *I'll Get There: It Better Be Worth the Trip* (John Donovan), at homosexuality; *A Bridge to Terabithia* (Katherine Paterson), at childhood death. But at the same time, these books also look at hope, perseverance, determination, strength, belief, and all-encompassing love.

Such books are often lumped together under the heading "relevant books." They are stories that utilize the strong, realistic material already familiar in other forms to many children. The worst of the "relevant" books merely exploit this material. The best explore. A sensitive exploration will lead the young reader into deeper insights and knowledge into problems, some of which he or she may share directly. And through these insights may come a gradual solving of some of the child's own problems.

Realistic novels

There are two things a writer must be aware of when beginning a realistic novel for young readers. First, ask yourself if you are writing this book for a moral purpose, to lead the young innocents away from the evils of which you write. Or are you simply telling a story? The former makes bad books, propaganda. The latter makes sense—and readers.

Second, it is almost a rule (that is, something which is only occasionally broken—successfully) that you use a child or a young person in telling the story. The reader finds it easier to identify with characters in the story if there is someone there of approximately the same age as the reader.

The two most important things in a realistic novel are character and plot.

At the "relevant" novel age (eight and up), young readers are not only quite capable of understanding in-depth characters; they actually demand them.

Often young critics are a great deal harsher with shallow characters than adult critics. In *The New York Times* several years ago, a teen-age novel about the drug scene was given eight reviews on a single page—seven were by teen-agers and one by an adult. The adult reviewer praised the book for its direct and honest approach to the "problem." The seven young readers crucified the book for the shallowness of its characters, who merely mouthed the author's moral purpose and had no lives of their own.

The fact that characters have a life of their own also means that *characters are plot*. A certain kind of person will respond to stimuli in certain ways. Putting a person under a microscope, like watching a paramecium on a slide, is essentially what a good novel does. The way your selected person moves is a goodly portion of plot. And so character = plot.

Before you do anything else, you must make your characters real to yourself. Catalogue their looks, their likes, their dislikes. Fill in a family history. Think of small anecdotes about their childhood—or infanthood, if they are still children. If you have a tape recorder and are a frustrated actor, speak your characters' dialogue into the tape to see if it sounds realistic.

You may never use half of what you sketch out, but it will make each character real to you. And then the character will have to be real to the reader.

Names and tags

Two "tricks" that may help you and your reader in identifying your characters are names and tags.

What's in a name? It can conjure up a character before the initial description, before a word is spoken, a deed acted. As John Cheever said in an interview in *Newsweek*: "I love making up names. One of the excitements of fiction is that if you get the right name, the person is alive."

Doesn't Scarlett O'Hara sound like an Irish-American spitfire? Cinderella's name places her well into the chimney corner. She probably changed it once she got her crown. Nero Wolfe brings to mind a dictatorial hunter. And if Captain Ahab wasn't as firmly and tragically wed to his white whale as his namesake was to Jezebel, then Melville misnamed him.

Shakespeare, one of the greatest name-callers in the literary world (Sir Toby Belch for comic effect; Peaseblossom, Cobweb, and Mustardseed for descriptive effect; Princess Perdita, the perfect name for a lost child) once said: "What's in a name? That which we call a rose/By any other name would smell as sweet." Perhaps. But if Toby Belch had been the name of Juliet's true love, I'm not so sure.

If names can help you establish a character before you have him firmly in mind, a tag for the character is what keeps you remembering him. A tag is some small action or figure of speech which one associates with a certain character. A peculiar twitch that belongs to no one else. For example, in real life I am a nail nibbler. I am sure that anyone describing me would mention this annoying habit. My daughter is always standing on her head or turning cartwheels—especially in crowded rooms. No character description of her would be complete without having her talk continually from an upside-down position. So, too, with fictional people.

Give your character a noticeable twitch or visible habit, and you make him or her memorable: a man who always rubs his eyebrow with his middle finger as he talks; or a girl who is continually twisting a strand of her hair; or a youngster who trys to be tough, and always ends a sentence with "Sez you, sez me." These are minor tricks, but they aid in character identity.

Once you have your character in your mind—looks, age, background, twitches, name, rank and serial number—you must introduce him to the audience quickly. In other words, before the end of the first chapter, you should establish this major character vividly in the reader's mind. But simple physical description will not do. (And pray, do not use the old mirror trick. That one is so outworn: "Sally looked into the mirror. A pretty blonde with a spray of freckles across her nose and a cast in one eye stared back.") Action is an important aid in delineating character. And action is an outgrowth of plot.

The two go together—character is plot and plot is character. And action is the key word for both.

Plot lines and outlines

Plot is always a very necessary element in a juvenile book, especially in a realistic book, where there are no fantastic elements to seduce the reader.

The plot—or story line—has sometimes been described as getting your character to the foot of the tree, getting him up the tree, and then figuring out how to get him down again. The length of time he is up the tree, dangling his feet, or falling from branch to branch like Pooh Bear on his disastrous honey-swiping trip, is a matter of style and diversions. But the main plot line is simple: to the tree, up the tree, and down.

Most writers, and I am among them, find it necessary to outline a novel completely. A long outline, chapter by chapter, often a page or more per chapter, means that I am never going to find myself up the wrong tree, or on the wrong branch at the wrong time. If the writer becomes lost in his own story, imagine how a reader will feel. It is most important that the writer is in control of the plot elements at all times. Like a juggler with apples and oranges twirling around, the author has to know just when to catch and when to let go, in order to keep things moving—and moving smoothly.

A funny thing about a realistic novel: It often takes on a life of its own. Instead of being the leader of a band of fascinating characters, the author suddenly finds himself running behind, desperately trying to catch up. If that happens, put aside the book, take up the outline again—and revise.

Style plays an understated role in a realistic novel. The extremely poetic or mannered style of a fantasy novel is anachronistic in a modern story. Straight reportage is usually the best way to write a relevant book.

But a book about teen-agers fairly aches to be written in the adolescent's own special language—slang. When that can of worms is opened, the problems that develop are legion. For nothing dates as quickly as slang. And nothing dates a relevant book faster than out-of-date slang. A teen-ager today would laugh at the slang of teen-agers of fifteen years ago. (When

I was a teen-ager, in the fifties, we said "neat-o" and "swing-ing" and "See you later, alligator.") My own children, ado-lescents of the eighties, say, "That's Ex!" and "Take off."

The major problem facing anyone who writes a relevant book is that of change—changing styles, changing values, changing language, changing interests. Nothing is more irrele-vant than a relevant book of the fifties or sixties.

These examples will prove the point. Here is a paragraph from Betty Cavanna's *Going on Sixteen,* published in 1946:

> "I'm going to do my hair in a page boy," Anne was going on, and immediately Julie could see that half the other girls at the table considered the possibility of also doing their hair in page boys. "There's a picture in one of mother's magazines of the neatest way!"

And then from *Academy Summer,* by Nan Gilbert, pub-lished fifteen years later, in 1961:

> Ben missed the sarcasm. "It sure would be. Gosh, a kid fresh from junior high wouldn't have any incentive at all to go out for athletics."
> "It might very well give him a complex."
> "You said it! No, Monroe High's been pretty swell, but now it's time to move into a bigger world."

No self-respecting teen-ager talks that way today—*neat, gosh, swell.* These books are dated by their dialogue, if not by their ideas. (*Going on Sixteen* looks at a girl whose parents are getting a divorce, and *Academy Summer* is about a group of musically talented teen-agers.) This is a perennial problem for authors of teen-age novels. Realistic novels are here today, gone tomorrow. Fantasy or historical fiction or period fiction (even when the history is only as old as the Roaring Twenties or the Depression or World War II) are here today, here tomorrow.

Underground and legitimate

Still, writing realistic fiction has some very positive rewards. It deals with subjects the children have heard of. They whisper about them in the dark corners of the cloak-room or read about them surreptitiously on bathroom walls. And wouldn't we rather have the children read about these subjects in a well-written novel that sheds lights and truth than learn them in the gutter? The underground subjects, simply because they are underground, are legitimate subjects for wonder. And children are the prize wonderers of us all. Yet, for years adults closed their eyes and ears to this small truth and assumed that children only knew—and wanted to know—about Peter Rabbit. When adults did that, they even denied memories of their own childhood. Quite simply, the children read these books and make an immediate identification with the characters. As one well-known editor put it, "Contemporary fiction is recognition fiction."

Some children *need* relevant books because, as Julius Lester has written, they have "to be an adult to cope with the world in which they live." He speaks from personal experience. He grew up in a ghetto in which "there were no Winnie the Pooh or Cinderella. . . . they have no meaning in the context of the . . . slum." Other children *need* relevant books simply because they have not had to be adults yet. The relevant books can lead these children to an understanding of other worlds, other people, other problems, other styles.

Children *desire* these books, too. Certainly in the past they have appropriated such books, making them their own. *A Tale of Two Cities, Oliver Twist, Robinson Crusoe, Moby Dick*— these "classics of childhood" were never meant for children at all. Yet the young readers adopted them and their messages of suffering, sacrifice, brutality—and love. In the present,

besides these old "blood-curdlers," young people continue
to adopt J. D. Salinger (*The Catcher in the Rye*) and Kurt
Vonnegut—though attempts to ban or burn these and other
writers' books continue. In fact, the American Library Association's Committee on Intellectual Freedom reported that
in the early 1980's incidents of book banning, removal of
specific titles from school and public libraries, and actual
book burnings across the country had increased at an alarm-
ing rate. Not only have authors of realistic books had their
books censored or banned, but consider the following as well:

> *A school board that banned a book sight unseen because of
> its title, *Making It With Mademoiselle,* only to learn later that
> this was a dressmaker's pattern book from the magazine
> *Mademoiselle.*
> *In Jacksonville, Florida, a Christmas play was banned because
> it used the word "pregnant" which they found too suggestive of
> sex education. Did Mary, one has to wonder, *find* the infant
> Jesus in the manger?
> *In Texas evangelists burned fairy tales, concluding that "Snow
> White" needed to be razed because "it introduces mirror gazing.
> There's a queen full of hate who turns herself into a wicked
> witch to destroy a teen-ager. That shows murder. . . ."
> *In Colorado a school board had *The Dictionary of American
> Slang* thrown out because a mother complained that she had
> found her child "chuckling over the dictionary."

If these were isolated incidents, we could laugh at them.
But they are not. And as authors we must be aware of the
subtle—and not so subtle—pressures placed upon us.

Books not initially meant for children can speak to them,
especially if the children recognize themselves in the situations and characters. Understanding this as a literary fact
of life, libraries now have shelves or sections set aside and
marked YA, Young Adult Books.

A study that was conducted by the National Assessment of Educational Progress showed that a large percentage of teen-agers rated literature "an important part" of their high school curriculum. Older teen-agers reported that they even believed the study of literature was important for practical reasons.

Children are not as frightened of reality as adults are. They are more likely just to accept it. Neither are they as frightened of the hobgoblins of their minds. They are ready and willing and able to tackle problems—their own and others. They realized long before the adults gave them credit for the realization that it's not all Peter Rabbit. They are looking for books that confirm that feeling.

Human beings are often liable to condescend to other animals, whose lives are often better organized than their own. . . .
—T. H. White

8

Lincoln's Doctor's Dog

THERE IS an old joke among publishers. It goes like this: Anything about Lincoln will sell a million copies. Anything about doctors does, too. And anything about dogs is the greatest seller of all. So . . . if we had a book entitled *Lincoln's Doctor's Dog*, we would really clean up!

Like any apocryphal tale, there is a lot of truth in it. Especially in the field of children's books, the animal story reigns supreme.

Children's books to most adults bring to mind soft bunnies, teddy bears, and other animals of the "cuddly" set. Or if the animal is too large to cuddle—like *Ferdinand* or *The Reluctant Dragon*—there are extenuating circumstances that make the animal if not cuddly at least pettable.

But animal stories are not all about cuddly or pettable animals. In fact, there are three distinct categories of animal books. (I am tempted to say good, bad, and Really Awful.) These categories are talking-animal stories, realistic animal stories, and scientific animal stories.

Animal stories are among the oldest stories in existence. In those once-upon-a-time days when people told stories around campfires, the animal was the character who conveyed the truth or dispensed the lies. The animals, closer to nature than man, had a direct relationship with the creator—whether that Creator was seen as Cronos, Jehovah, Odin, or any other.

The first "authors" to use animals in their stories were the primitive storytellers. From there to the medieval fabliau was but a short step through Aesop. Bestiaries perverted and added to known animals, melding the real and the unreal with fantastic abandon. By La Fontaine's time, the animal stories had left all innocence behind and had become satirical fables. Then animals fell into disrepute as man concentrated his scientific and literary efforts on industrializing the world.

When Anna Sewell wrote *Black Beauty* in 1877, with great philanthropic intent, a new kind of animal story was born— the realistic animal tale. No longer were animal stories merely a means to clothe man's foibles in fur and feathers. In Mrs. Sewell's tale, there was no doubt which was the man and which the beast. Man was cruel and ignoble while the horse was noble and long (very long) suffering.

In 1896, close on the heels of *Black Beauty,* the third strain of animal story was begun with Sir Charles G. D. Roberts' *Earth Enigmas.* His stories were *super* realistic and often excluded any human characters. In Roberts' tales, the animals are motivated by habit and by instinct, not by greed for power, vanity, shyness, or love.

Animal tales in general are probably the single greatest category in children's books. The animal story spans all ages —from the tiniest picture book to full-length novels. There is not one publisher who does not have a horse or dog book somewhere on his present or past list, usually several of both. Plus ant books, rabbit books, toad and frog books, mouse books, elephant books, pig books, dragon books, and even unicorn books.

Talking-animal books

The talking-animal book is the delight of the young readers and the bane of the editor's existence. As an editor, I turned down more talking pussy cats and puppy dogs than I care to remember. As a teacher I discouraged a talking prune story, too, which is an extension of the same problem.

The "problem" is that usually these stories suffer from "the cutes." Children know, without being told, that animals do not really talk (except, perhaps, on Christmas Eve), so when a book contains a talking animal, they respond to it as they do any fantasy or folk tale. From the writer's point of view, then, these books must abide by the rules of the genre—folk tale or fantasy, whichever it may be. Only in these talking animal tales can the animals respond as prototypical humans.

If you want to write about an animal that has feelings and strong emotional responses, you had better realize that you are writing a fantasy story. For not only do animals *not* talk, they do not have human emotions. If, as T. H. White claims, their lives are better organized than our own, it is on a simpler scale: direct responses to stimuli rather than the tortuous mind-turnings of humankind.

However, even if in your fantasy the animal(s) talks, keep one thing in mind. No matter how well it enunciates its words or how deep its emotions, remember its animal size, shape and special interests. If it is a toad, as in my own *Hobo Toad and the Motorcycle Gang,* then it cannot suddenly bend steel bars with its hands, or fly. In that story, the toad saves the day by using his marvelous tongue—flicking open the knots in the ropes that bind his companions with the same ease with which he flicks flies. If the animal is a spider, as in E. B. White's *Charlotte's Web*, it helps out by spinning messages in its web rather than swimming under water or carving up the opposition with a knife. If the animal is not helpful, of what use is it in the first place—except to be *cute?*

This then is the first question a writer must ask himself before he embarks on a talking-animal story—is the animal necessary to the tale? Why not simply make it a human being and be done with it? If your answer is "Because an animal is cuter," or "I just felt like putting it there," or a similar response, it is time to rethink your premise.

Take a look at some of the great stories with animals that talk: *Peter Rabbit* and *Squirrel Nutkin* by Beatrix Potter; *The Wind in the Willows,* by Kenneth Grahame; Kipling's *Jungle Book.* They have necessary animals that talk. They also avoid the three major traps of this kind of book—triviality, sentimentality, and melodrama.

Realistic animal stories

The second kind of animal book—the realistic animal book —began, as I have said, with the nineteenth-century *Black Beauty.* Straight on through the sentimental Jack London, Albert Terhune, and Walter Farley stories, the animals' hearts break as regularly as clockwork.

These stories are realistic—to a point. The animals growl or grunt or gobble rather than talk. They do not wear clothes or mess about in boats. Yet, the authors, romantics at heart, often endow their "dumb" animals with human emotions.

In the realistic animal story, the animal may be a hero, like *Bob, Son of Battle* (Alfred Ollivant), or an anti-hero like *Old One-Toe* (Michel-Aimé Baudouy), or a super-hero like the

Black Stallion (Walter Farley). But these episodic adventure stories have in common noble and often suffering animals.

What might sound trite and sentimental in a human story can sound right when it is a realistic animal tale. We still invest animals with that closer-to-the-creation nobility. Children, even more than adults, respond to animals in this way.

The keynote for these books is plot: fast-paced adventures tumbling over one another, hair-breadth escapes. Each chapter should end on the cliff's edge, like the old "Perils of Pauline" movies. If folk tales have to have . . . *and then* in every paragraph, these longer books—often novel-length of 30,000–60,000 words—should have . . . *and then* at every chapter's end.

Scientific animal stories

The scientific animal story is relatively new. Less than a hundred years old, this type of story is growing fast but should be attempted only by authors who really understand animal life. Writers cannot successfully fake a scientific animal story, for every fact, every movement the animal makes in one of these books has to be authentic and realistic.

Often the authors of these books are zoologists, biologists, veterinarians, or animal breeders. All are ardent wildlife observers. For example, Alfred Milotte and his wife spent over a year in Africa watching hippos, most of that time in a glass-fronted underwater tank, photographing the large animals for a Disney film. Their book, *The Story of a Hippopotamus*, benefits from their close and patient observations. Sterling North's *Rascal* was so popular because the author had been a first-hand witness to the raccoon events he described. On the younger level, Robert M. McClung's life-cycle stories like *Spike, The Story of a Whitetail Deer* and David Stemple's *High Ridge Gobbler* are both story and accurate observation.

Sometimes in these scientific animal stories, the actual events are true and reported exactly. *Born Free* is an example of this. But in *The Story of a Hippopotamus*, the story of the life of one particular hippopotamus is actually a composite of a number of hippos the Milottes observed.

The success of these stories sometimes depends on the obscurity of the animal. In a market satiated with cats and dogs, the real life story of a star-nosed mole, a vampire bat, or a harpy eagle might more readily find a publisher and audience.

Hurdles

The animal story category is as wide as the world. It ranges from the talking lion lying down with the lamb to the scientifically accurate lion devouring its woolly companion. But there are two major obstacles between the would-be writer of animal stories and his or her intended audience.

The first is the editor who, after twenty-two successive talking-kitty stories and a talking-prune tale, refuses to look at another anthropomorphic story, whether the animal talks and walks around on two feet or is rather scientifically drawn. There are editors who hate the idea of animal tales, and in general, it is best to query first.

The second obstacle is symbolized by the librarian who said, after I recommended two absolutely delightful mouse stories to her—*Time To Go House,* by Newbery winner Walter Edmonds and *The Great Cheese Conspiracy,* by Jean Van Leeuwen—"I can't lay out any more money for another mouse tale. I just bought two." The two she pointed to me were *Mousekin's Golden House* (Edna Miller) and a scientific textbook about field and house mice. None of the four books was at all similar. They were aimed at different ages, different reading levels, different interests, and different pocketbooks. But they *were* all about mice. And so she rested her case.

*The world is wide. Everything in it can be
used to make books for children.*
                                    —Taro Yashima

9

Short Takes

THE ANCIENT art of poetry was sacred. That, in a nutshell,
is why it is so hard to lead children to poetry today. We adults
still have a poetry-is-sacred attitude. Like so many things that
are sacred to adults, children won't touch it with a ten-foot
pole.

What most adults forget is that children are themselves
natural poets. In the past ten years, anthologists have suddenly been discovering this. Richard Lewis has collected two
beautiful volumes of poems written by children: *Miracles* and
The Wind and the Rain. The poems in these books breathe
a freshness of language and vision that many a would-be poet
would love to cultivate.

Poem, verse, and jingle-jingle-jingle

Poetry for children comes either in collections or as a jingly-
verse picture book. Both are difficult to sell. The reason is
that both are difficult to write—well.

If you are interested in poetry collections, that is collecting other people's poems, then you must start with a theme. The theme may be used as open-ended as *poems by children* or *poems about the earth* or as closed as *poems about dogs.*

Next you must start collecting the poems. Read more than other collections; read through the entire lifework of single great poets. Delve into the newest small quarterlies for your material, as well as into old children's magazines. But be sure you use quality—not just thematic adherence—as your guide.

Remember, children do not want just "winky little daisy flower" poetry, as we call that bumpity-bump verse in our family. Children want strong, firm, palpable poems. The kind of poems Archibald MacLeish meant when he wrote, "A poem should not mean/but be." Furthermore, as Eve Merriam, one of the best poets around for children *and* adults, says, in a book of the same name, "It doesn't have to rhyme."

If you are interested in a collection of your own poetry, you should already be a well-published poet. Your poems may have been published in small university quarterlies or mass magazines, in esoteric scholarly periodicals or *Jack and Jill.* But it is next to impossible to have a book of poems for young readers published with no prior reputation or record of publication in the field.

Again, if you are going to submit a volume of your own verse for publication, it helps if it is thematic. A new Mother Goose? Clyde Watson's *Father Fox's Pennyrhymes* is an excellent example. *Woody and Me,* by Mary Neville, one of those rare "first books" of poetry, is about two brothers— Woody and his younger sibling (the "me" of the title). Lilian Moore's *See My Lovely Poison Ivy,* with a Halloween theme, is a charmer, and funny, too.

Here are some thematic suggestions for poetry collections if you enjoy writing verse: Seasonal Songs, Everyday Prayers, Night Songs, Street Cries, Animals I'd Like To Meet.

A good poem for children captures in a very small instant something a child recognizes, something honest, emotion-laden, that makes a child say, "That's right. I know how that feels." Or a delightful word-playing joke that repeats and repeats in a child's head. The latter is what makes Mother Goose rhymes so successful: the rhythms, the bounce, the music that rings like a bell in the child's soul.

But the poems do not have to *begin* as children's poetry to be successful as poems for a child. You do not talk down in a poem any more than you would in another kind of children's book. Again—quality. Many of the Mother Goose rhymes were first and foremost political satire. And children have throughout the centuries taken great poems as their own: Shakespeare's "Full Fathom Five," and Donne's "Go, and Catch a Falling Star," as well as poems by Dylan Thomas, Yeats, e. e. cummings, and Roethke.

Another area in which a poetic individual can write is in translation. Robert Wyndham's *Chinese Mother Goose Rhymes* is a beautiful example of how a curious mind and a poetic sensibility can lead to a very new, very different, and very beautiful book. Barbara Cooney's *Le Hibou et la Poussiquette,* is, of course, a turnabout of translation.

The important thing to remember is that jingly verse, winky daisy flower poetry rhythms and wrenched rhymes are not necessarily poetry. Certainly they are not the only poems that should be available for children. If children can write better poems than that for themselves, they deserve the very best from the adult poet, too.

Vocabulary

When I first began writing for children, I inadvertently came upon a "word list" sent out by a publishing company for would-be juvenile authors. Two pages printed in very large type contained the entire beginning reader's vocabulary allowed in the books—361 words. For the *beginning* beginner (whatever that means!) 181 words.

The introduction to the list, written in a simplified English even a beginning author would understand, spelled out the ground rules for writing juveniles for this well-known publisher.

First of all, the introduction reassured us, these were the words in the leading first-grade textbooks, words which the children already knew by sight. And with that sanction, the rules began. Authors were warned against *-ed* and *-ing* and *-er* endings. They were cautioned about contractions. And they were absolutely forbidden the use of *possessives*. I have wondered ever since whether the list people actually believed that children of early reading age do not understand possessives. Or were the list authors, perhaps, attempting a moral lesson?

I puzzled over the 361 words for a long time, trying to imagine the kind of story I could write with such an imposed structure—or stricture—and came up with nothing at all. I felt like a potter asked to make a bowl with an ounce of clay, or a woodworker ordered to create a table with a splinter.

Of course, there was always the possibility that I was lacking in imagination. So I turned to that master of imaginative sense and nonsense, Lewis Carroll. Turning to the first page of *Alice in Wonderland*, I read:

> Alice was beginning to get very tired of sitting by her sister on the bank, and of having nothing to do; once or twice she had peeped into the book her sister was reading, but it had no pictures or conversation in it, "and what is the use of a book," thought Alice, "without pictures or conversation."

Clearly it would never do. There were over twenty words not sanctioned by the list, not to mention perfectly good words ruined by -*ed* and -*ing* endings. Without a doubt, *Alice* was not for today's young readers.

But I remembered vividly my first reading of *Alice*. I knew that, given the proper vocabulary, children in the second half of the twentieth century would love the book. So, list in hand, I removed the offending words.

> Alice was to get very of sit by her on the, and of no thing to do; once or she had into the book her was read, but it had no or in it, "and what is the of a book," thought Alice, "with out or."

Heavens—jabberwocky!

My duty was clear. I must render *Alice* readable for young readers today. Obviously, deleting words was not what the list-makers had in mind. I would rewrite the classic, using only the approved words, substituting them for any of the forbidden vocabulary.

> Alice began to get very sleepy as she sat by her mother by the water with not a thing to do. One or two times she had looked into the book her mother read, but it had no paint or talk in it, "and what good is a book," thought Alice, "with no paint or talk."

It was readable. Even understandable. Yet something was lost in translation—style, fluidity of language, a poetry of sound, and occasionally even the intent of the author.

It is lost any time you try to write a book for a child with a proscribed and prescribed vocabulary. What is a proscribed vocabulary anyway? In *The New England Primer*, there was a word list for young Puritan readers that included such words as *fornication, vile,* and *sloth*. None of those words were within a mile of my twentieth-century list. So a proscribed vocabulary has something to do with easy words and something to do with moral lessons, too.

The classic example of the idiocy of limited vocabularies (or "word leveling") was read at an American Library Association meeting some years ago. Written by children's book editor Ann Durrell, it was a parody of an easy-to-read vervion of the classic, *Jane Eyre:*

> This is Jane.
> Hello Jane.
> Jane is poor.
> Her dress is poor.
> Her shoes are poor.
> Her hat is poor.
> Poor Jane.
>
> This is Mr. Rochester.
> Hello Mr. Rochester.
> Mr. Rochester is rich.
> He has a big house.
> He has a big dog.
> He has a big horse.
> He has a big secret.
> What is Mr. Rochester's secret?
> Jane cannot guess the secret.
> Can you guess the secret?
>
> This is Mrs. Rochester.
> Hello Mrs. Rochester.
> Mrs. Rochester is crazy.
> She has a candle.
> The candle is lighted.
> Mrs. Rochester can laugh.
> She laughs: ha ha ha.
>
> RUN JANE RUN.

So my answer to the perennial question about the proper vocabulary for a children's book is this: use the word which is the right word for the occasion, whether it is a one-letter, two-letter, three-letter, twenty-eight-letter, or four-letter word. If the child already knows the word, there is no problem. (After all, beginning readers already have a speaking vocabulary of several *thousand* words.) If the child has to learn the word, so much the better.

As Tolkien has said about children: "Their books like their clothes should allow for growth, and their books at any rate should encourage it."

However, there is a certain kind of beginning-to-read book known in the trade as the "easy reader" and since there is certainly a demand for this kind of book, it needs to be mentioned. These are books that are written in shorter sentences and, while the vocabulary is usually not controlled with a word list, it is true that the words *tend* to be more easily comprehended by a new reader. (Keep in mind, though, that a 7-year-old can more easily read and understand a word such as *brontosaurus* than *slough*; in this case familiarity breeds content.)

Many publishers have specific series of easy readers— Harper & Row has its *I Can Read,* Dutton has its *Smart Cats,* Coward McCann its *Break of Day,* to name a few. There are also specific science read-alone series (Crowell), history read-alone series (Harper) and the famous Random House beginner books.

What these books have in common is that they are aimed for the boys and girls who have just broken the code of reading and want to read something *interesting.* The best of these books are not only interesting, they are marvelous reading: Arnold Lobel's *Frog and Toad* books, Betty Boegehold's Pippa Mouse books, the Hobans' Frances the badger books, Sue Alexander's *Witch, Goblin, Ghost* stories, Fritz and Aliki Brandenberg's field mice family tales, and, of course, the ever-popular *Little Bear* books by Elsie Minerik.

An important trick of the easy-reading trade is writing in "breath spaces." Once children can sound out letters and read words, the hardest thing is for them to make sense of the sentences. Punctuation still lies far down the road as a consistent skill. Children read a word—or phrase—at a time. But what constitutes a phrase? Any group of words sitting together on a line *looks* like a phrase. So they use that for a guide. And if the phrase they see goes like this:

> Jack and Jill went up

they read it just that way. Writing in "breath spaces" teaches them the skill of pausing at the correct moment.

When I wrote the first of my Star Warts books, *Commander Toad in Space,* I set the story on the page as if it were a poem, in the way it should be read aloud:

> Long ships fly
> between the stars,
> Outside each porthole
> worlds wink off and on.
> There is one ship,
> one mighty ship,
> long and green,
> that goes across the skies.

It is impossible to read that story "incorrectly." Never mind that it has some big words—*porthole* and, later on, *commander, galaxies, alien.* They are all outer-space words and a child who wants to read a science fiction easy reader is already primed for them.

The middle-aged child

Somewhere in-between the picture-book-age child and the Young Adult is a fairie creature known in library circles as "The Middle-Aged Child." The 8–12s, as they are also called, are problem children for editors and for librarians. According to editors, no one ever writes for that age group. Yet every editor is asking for such books. It is the age when, as the old song goes, "a person is too old to play with dollies, too young to join the follies."

But these children have a very special reading need. In Anne Carroll Moore's words, they are "reading for life." These are the children about to step off into the great adventure of adulthood. If they are fed trashy books, hack books, books written with our old friend "benign indifference," those books of lies, then their young lives might be warped. It is *that* serious.

These are children who are making their own reading choices. They go to libraries and pick out their own books, without guidance of parents or librarians, but with a great deal of nudging from their friends. To give them a choice of "the lesser of two evils" when it comes to books may, in a way, be preparing them for life. But it is not really the way to impart a lesson.

The books needed for the middle-aged child might be best described as picture novels, for they lie between the totally illustrated books and the totally word books. They range from fantasy on a small scale through realistic fiction of the past and present. There is special emphasis on *curriculum-oriented* books.

Curriculum-oriented means that these books can fulfill a teacher's outside-the-classroom reading needs. They cover topics, or take place in countries or during historical times that children are currently studying. Sometimes an editor will have on hand the curriculum of major school systems: California, New York, Texas, Michigan. The editor can then consult the curriculum to see if the manuscript she is interested in—say a novel for young readers about an Indian girl or an adventure of a young Quaker boy in William Penn's day or the story of an African boy of the Watusi a hundred years

ago—can be promoted as being perfect for the fifth-grade curriculum.

The problem with most middle-aged books is that they have
middle-age spread. Instead of beginning with a story idea or
a fascinating character, they begin with a moral or an idea to
teach or a prod from the school curriculum.

Technically, these books run between thirty to one hundred
typewritten pages. Once a book is accepted, it is given an
age-grouping: 7–9, 8–12, 9–13, 10 and up, etc. These are
rather arbitrary labels and assigned by the editor in conjunc-
tion with the sales department.

There are two rather silly and often violated "rules" about
this kind of book. Like any "rule," once you have mastered
it and understand where it springs from, you can break it
with impunity. The first is that the child-hero in your middle-
age book must be at least as old or slightly older than the
reader. It is often noted that children like to read about someone a bit older—never younger—than themselves. On the
other hand, the beautiful and moving book about the death
of a sibling, *The Magic Moth*, by Virginia Lee, violates this
cardinal rule by having the point of view of the story belong
to the six-year-old brother.

Cardinal rule number two is that girls will read boys' books
but boys will not read girls' books. The corollary to that rule
is, that's O.K.—boys don't read much, anyway. If this is a
rule, it is changing, and it is up to the writers to speed up
the change. If there are more exciting adventure stories in
which the girls are the actors instead of the acted upon, the
rescuers rather than the rescuees, just as smart and as active
as their brothers, then this "natural" division will break down.
Boys like Scott O'Dell's *Island of the Blue Dolphins* just as
much as girls do. *The Wizard of Oz* is a perennial favorite of
boys *and* girls. Also, *Alice in Wonderland*, Louise Fitzhugh's
Harriet the Spy, and Jean C. George's *Julie of the Wolves*
have this in common—uncommon and active young heroines.

The important thing to remember about middle-age books is that there is an open market for them. Editors are actively seeking these books. Every marketing list underlines the editor's desire to receive them. "Send me 8–12s," the editors plead. "I'm always open to new writers in the middle group," they say.

And as a happy P.S., these are the children who write the most letters to the authors about their favorite books.

Paperbacks bring readers back

In the days of the chapbooks, lower-class paperback novels like *Jack the Giant Killer* sold for a penny and a determined child reader might sneak one home (for Mother and Father disapproved of such reading). When I was growing up, paperback books for adults (there were none for children) were mostly bang-bang-shoot-'em-ups or slightly risqué novels like *The Amboy Dukes,* by Irving Shulman, that we earmarked and passed from friend to friend, actually reading them in the bathroom because not even the most enterprising and censurious mother would track you down there.

But today paperbacks are a different animal altogether, and especially different and new are paperbacks for children.

Almost every major publisher today has—or is in the process of developing—a line of juvenile paperbacks. Dell was a pioneer in the field. Its Yearling Books for the younger and Laurel Leaf Library for older children are very popular. (*Charlotte's Web,* a Yearling reprint, has sold over a million copies.) Viking Seafarer books, the first well-produced paperback reprints of quality picture books, has brought out such perennial favorites as the Madeline books (Ludwig Bemelmans), *Andy and the Lion* (James Daugherty), and *Journey Cake, Ho!* (Sawyer and McCloskey). Almost all the books published in paperback are reprints of time-tested favorites.

The publisher first puts its own backlist into paper before reaching out elsewhere. The problems, of course, are legion with softcover books: the book has a shorter span of life; the paper, the binding, the inks used are less costly and, consequently, less durable. The awful truth is that the books fall apart after a few readings by children. That is why libraries are slow to order paperbacks in quantity. Since traditionally libraries have been the mainstay of the children's book field, publishers are loath to put all their eggs—their *original* eggs, that is—in the paperback basket.

But paperback originals for children and young people are growing in number and importance. Not all of these are marketed to the general public or sold in bookstores. Schools use them in increasing numbers, not only as book club editions distributed through the schools, but in libraries and as texts. A growing number of publishers are bringing out paperback originals, fiction and nonfiction, but with the frequent changes, it is well to check before submitting a manuscript. Some of these publishers are: Avon (Camelot, Flare); Bantam (Dark Forces); Dell (Yearling, Laurel Leaf, Twilight); Scholastic (Wildfire, Vagabond, Wishing Star, Pretzel).

Magazines for children

From 1873 to 1940, there lived a publishing phenomenon known as *St. Nicholas*. It was a magazine for children that in its heyday published such authors as Louisa May Alcott, Frank Stockton, L. Frank Baum, Bret Harte, Frances Hodgson Burnett, Joel Chandler Harris and others. In its pages, the stories we associate with our own childhood first saw light: Kipling's *The Jungle Book*, Lucretia Hale's *The Peterkin Papers*, Mary Mapes Dodge's *Hans Brinker, or the Silver Skates*, Howard Pyle's *King Arthur*, Joel Harris's *Uncle Re-*

mus Stories, Louisa May Alcott's *Under the Lilacs,* and *Jack and Jill*—to name a few.

Since that time, there has been a proliferation of magazines for young readers. But none has ever come up with the wit, the style, the literacy, and the fantastic amounts of pure genius of *St. Nicholas.*

Nowadays, children's magazines seem to follow a style best described as Late Eclectic: a few stories, a factual article or two, a few poems (mostly jingly verse), a game to learn, some crafts and things-to-do features, a simple-minded song, and some puzzles and/or riddles.

A complete list of magazines for young readers and their editorial requirements can be found in *The Writer* magazine. Also, *Literary Market Place,* available in reference departments of most public libraries, includes a selected list of these publications. The following are among the best known and most widely read:

Jack and Jill (ages 4–10), 1100 Waterway Blvd., Indianapolis, Ind. 46202. One of the most popular, it features stories for beginning readers set in large type, some verse. Fiction from 300–1500 words, factual articles. Pays on publication.

Humpty Dumpty (ages 3–7). A publication of Parents Magazine Enterprises, 52 Vanderbilt Ave., New York, N.Y. 10017. Uses three kinds of stories: 1. Picture stories, usually on assignment; 2. Read-Aloud Stories up to 900 words; 3. Tell-Me Stories to be read by parents to child, up to 1000 words. Pays on acceptance.

Highlights for Children (ages 3–11), 803 Church St., Honesdale, Pa. 18431. Regularly uses stories under 1000 words, humor or struggle or self-sacrifice preferred. Pays 6¢ word and up on acceptance.

Cricket (ages 6–10), Open Court Publishing Co., Box 599, LaSalle, Ill. 61301. Regularly uses stories and articles, 200 to 2,000 words, and poems up to 100 lines in length. Pays 25¢ a word for prose, and $3 a line for poetry.

Cobblestone (ages 8-12), Peterborough, NH 03458. A history magazine that uses stories, articles, poems on specific themes. A list of themes for a year ahead will be sent on request. Enclose a self-addressed, stamped envelope.

*Each good book calls forth a different response
from an editor.*

—Jean Karl

10

Follow Your Manuscript

THE MOMENT of truth is at hand. You have finished your manuscript and typed it, double-space, and made at least one carbon. Now you are ready to send it off to—to whom?

Do you send it to any old publisher, pick the first name on the list of juvenile publishers—Abingdon? Or the last one—Windmill Books? Do you send it to the editor named there or the publisher? Or to your best friend, who is a typist in the royalty department? Do you send it to an agent?

Read this chapter before you do anything. It may save you time, it may save you money, and it may save your soul—or at least your soul as a writer.

Basics in marketing

The first thing you must know—and believe—is that no matter how you send your manuscript, *it will be read*. Even if you address it, "To Whom It May Concern" and forget the ubiquitous stamped, self-addressed envelope; whether you send it First Class, as I do, or by Special Fourth Class Manuscript Rate, it will be read. And whether you send it with a covering letter two pages long or no letter at all, it will be read. It will be read by the appropriate person, and, if necessary, returned. Despite reports to the contrary, editors do not use manuscripts as paper towels, lighter fuel, or coffee cup coasters. Neither do they send manuscripts back to the authors unread. (Every year manuscripts arrive at publishing offices with some of the pages turned upside down or stapled together by untrusting authors as a test to see if the book *is* read. At Random House/Knopf, when I was an editor there, we used to turn the pages upside down again when we were finished reading, because we were angry at the gratuitous insult.)

Editors know that authors are the lifeblood of a publishing house. Without the author, where would a publishing company be? Probably manufacturing diapers or copper washers or rifle sights—not books.

But . . . and it is that *but* which you must beware of . . . there are many ways to read a manuscript. There are many ways to handle a manscript, and many ways to accept and/or reject a manuscript. What this chapter will do is instruct you in the way to send out your manuscript to guarantee it the best reading by the most qualified person in the shortest amount of time with the least amount of return and heartbreak for all involved. That is not a small order.

First you must study the market carefully. For example, Philomel (Putnam Publishing Group) has a smallish list, with only three or four picture books per season. Doubleday has many. Franklin Watts publishes several nonfiction books every year. Atheneum emphasizes fiction. Nonfiction books are a mainstay of the Random House list, but you cannot find any at Bradbury.

Studying the market can be done in several ways, but the easiest of these is to write away for the publishers' catalogues. Visits to your local library or bookstore are also helpful, as are talks to the librarian or bookseller.

Next you might take time to send a query letter. This is especially time-saving for a nonfiction project or an historical or period novel, adventure, or sports story. An editor will not want to take on a project or novel too similar to one already published or in the works.

A simple query letter might look like this:

Dear Mr. G:

I am working on a book about the history and lore of bells tentatively entitled, *Ring Out: A Book of Bells*. It is for the 8–12 age group and will include stories and songs about bells as well as historical material.

There are only eight books on bells that are in print today, of which two are juveniles. The juveniles are for a much younger age than the book I am writing.

My writing background includes twenty published books for young readers and many magazine and newspaper articles.

If you are interested, I would be pleased to send you a full outline and the first chapter of my proposed book.

Sincerely,

This kind of letter is sure to elicit a quick response from an editor. It explains the project simply, outlines the competition, specifies the writer's expertise (or specific familiarity with the material) and finally demonstrates that there is, indeed, something more "on paper" for the editor to read. Query letters may be sent to any number of editors at the same time. When their answers arrive, you may judge by the degree of interest, which one would be most sympathetic to the book. Although multiple queries are more acceptable than in the past, beginners should be aware that some publishers still have some objection to them.

A query letter is a shortcut, because it will be answered in a relatively short time—possibly in days, certainly no longer than a few weeks. Manuscripts quite often are kept months by a publishing company—and then rejected. But query letters are answered sooner.

However, do not send a query letter about a fantasy novel. They are useless. They can never give the flavor, style, or feeling of a book. Can you imagine the letter Rev. Charles Dodgson [Lewis Carroll] might send?

Dear Sirs:
    Under a pseudonym I have written a story about a little girl who falls down a rabbit hole and has a series of adventures with a pack of cards.
    Are you interested?

                Sincerely,
                s/Charles Dodgson

Dear Rev. Dodgson:
    No thanks!

                Sincerely,
                s/Any Publisher

If you receive a letter from the editor or assistant editor showing interest, address your manuscript to that same person. It means continuity; that person will most likely remember your query and will look forward to receiving and reading the script.

Rules for submission

When you send out that manuscript, whether in response to a letter or on an educated guess, remember these six important rules.

1. *Always type the manuscript,* whether it is a one-page picture story or a 200-page novel. An editor's job in part consists of reading hundreds of manuscripts every year. He will not take time to look at a handwritten story, even if you have a Master's Degree in calligraphy. *Not typed, not read* is the rule. Double-space the manuscript, leaving wide margins on both sides and on both the top and bottom. It gives your manuscript a professional look. Also be sure it has as few corrections and scribblings-in in ink or pencil as possible. A heavy weight (20 lb.) erasable bond is what I use.

2. *Be sure your name and address are on the title page.* Also, number your pages consecutively. This sounds like an idot's rule, but, believe me, it is possible to forget. If by accident a manuscript is dropped, it can be reassembled with ease if it is numbered. With hundreds of manuscripts going through the editor's hands each year, the laws of probability point out that at least once or twice two manuscripts are going to get mashed together. Somehow it always seems to be *your* manuscript. Putting your name on each page and numbering your pages reduces the possibility of total loss.

3. *Always keep at least one carbon or Xerox copy.* Two are preferable. Although this may seem an idiot's rule, I know many bright new writers who do not make copies. It is always the manuscript they do not have a copy of (because it is only "two short pages") that is lost in the mail, in the mailroom, or behind a bookcase in the editor's office. Also, keep carbons of all your correspondence, not only as a record of where your manuscript has been, but also for posterity. Years from now, when you are rich and famous, someone will want to publish your letters. Even if that never happens, you can always enjoy the "true" story of the travels of your manuscript after your belief in it has been vindicated. Recently I checked back over the correspondence of my book, *The Em-*

peror and the Kite. (I keep a journal, too, recording each book's progress and my thoughts about it.) I reveled in the letter from one editor who turned the book down because it was "just not a real story." The book was a Caldecott Honor Book, a Lewis Carroll Shelf winner, an ALA Notable Book, and one of *The New York Times* "Best Books of the Year." Revenge *is* sweet.

4. *Keep a card file of your manuscript's travels* so that you do not send it back where it has already been. This may not be necessary with only one manuscript out, but once you have several manuscripts traveling around to the publishers, it is impossible to keep all the back-and-forths in your head. Since each trip out may entail up to three or four months, it would be a waste of valuable time to send a manuscript to someone who has already rejected it. The editor will not get to it sooner because he has already seen it. He will simply take two months to reject it all over again.

5. *Never submit the same manuscript to more than one publisher at a time.* Multiple submissions are frowned upon by almost everyone in the juvenile field. The usual reason given is that if two publishers both want to publish the book, you are in trouble. Actually, you are then in the enviable position of being a seller in a seller's market, but nevertheless, setting up an auction of your manuscript is bad form—and you could stand to lose *both* publishers.

6. *A cover letter is not necessary.* But if you do send one, remember that *less is more.* That means that the less you write, the more the editor will appreciate it. A cover letter should include only such information as is important to the understanding of the manuscript: if it is the only book of its kind, or the reason that you are the perfect person to have written it. No extraneous biographical material, please.

The editor does not need to know your age, financial status, or the fact that your grandchildren loved the book. However, if you have had something published before, if you are a teacher or a librarian, you might add that to your letter.

Agents

Now for a small detour. To agent or not to agent, that is the question. In fact, it is a question that has been asked so often, the word *agent* has become a transitive verb.

The problem is that there are so very few agents who really know the juvenile field. To find out the names of the ones who might be of some help, write to the Society of Authors' Representatives, 101 Park Avenue, New York, New York 10017. (Be sure to enclose a self-addressed stamped envelope.) The SAR will supply, upon request, a list of the reputable agents in the business. What a new writer must beware of are the agents who charge a stiff reader's fee. (They often adverstise.) Their aim is to make money *from* an author, not to make money *for* an author.

The problem is that finding or getting an agent is just as hard (if not harder) than getting a publisher. Since there are very few agents for children's books, the ones there are are most selective.

Is an agent necessary? I have one, but many famous and successful juvenile authors do not. There are authors who swear by them—and authors who swear at them. My agent is my ombudsman to the publisher, as conversant with copyright and contractual matters as a lawyer, a firm believer in my literary talents, and also a long-beloved friend. But I know other writers who dislike their agents with a passion exceeded only by their agents' dislike of them. They are bound strictly by business ties. The answer to the question, "Is an agent necessary?" is "No." Not unless you feel they are. Then they are indispensable.

What use is an agent? An agent is on top of the publishing scene, knows which editors have recently moved to new companies or have had companies fold up under them. The agent knows an editor's special likes and dislikes, a company's latest needs. The agent knows which publishing companies are the most reputable, produce the most luscious books, have the best sales distribution, treat their authors with the most respect, advertise their products most heavily, and are the most trustworthy in all their financial dealings. The agent also has contacts with European publishers, movie companies, TV studios, radio producers, record companies. The agent understands the fine print on a contract and will fight for the highest advance and royalty terms for the author, the best secondary rights, and the most generous general terms. The agent also takes 10% to 15%. Of everything. Artists' representatives get up to 50%.

The editorial process

Once the manuscript is on its way to the publishing house, forget it. Begin immediately on a new story or book or poem. This is the professional attitude. As Phyllis Whitney so aptly puts it: "No vacations between stories." If you are working hard on something else, you will never notice how long it is taking you to hear from the publisher.

It is going to take a long time, too. Anywhere from six weeks to four months is normal. This is why:

When the manuscript reaches the publishing house, it is catalogued in by either a secretary or a manuscript clerk. Often you will receive a postcard stating that the company has received your script and is not responsible for the safety of same. Then the manuscript is placed in one of three piles.

If it is a manuscript from one of the editor's own authors or from a famous author published elsewhere, it goes into pile number one. Pile number one will be read by the editor him- or herself, probably within a matter of days or at most weeks.

If it is a manuscript from a respected agent or from a published though not well-known author, or from a friend of a friend, it goes into pile number two. This pile is usually read by a secondary person first—an assistant editor, a manuscript reader, even an outside reader. Then a report on the script is written. It may be as short as, "A tale about two monkeys in Jataka who outwit a crocodile. It is based on an old folk motif. Author is Indian and has written this with wit and style. Suggest second reading." Or the report may run several pages. Then the editor reads the manuscript, keeping in mind the report of the first reader. So, if your best friend *is* a typist in the royalty department, be sure to send it through her. It will land your manuscript in pile number two. (And be sure to mention this friend in any covering letter.)

The third pile is called the *slush* pile. That is short for "unsolicited." (One company, though, once tried calling their slush pile the Discovery Pile.) All other manuscripts, those that come in without any significant pedigrees attached, go into pile number three. Slush it is called, and like slush it is often treated. (And to be fair, slush it often is. I remember vividly one manuscript from my days as a manuscript clerk. It came from the slush pile and went:

> A.
> AB.
> ABC.
> ABCD.   etc.

It came in without illustrations but with an accompanying letter about the author's need for quick money.)

Make no mistake—each manuscript, even in the slush pile, is read to the degree to which it deserves. And no amount of hopscotching from pile to pile will make an editor buy an unacceptable manuscript. Excellent slush pile stories will get a second reading by the next man or woman up the editorial totem. And if it is liked by the second reader, slush will be passed on to the editor. There are, every year, a few books published from the slush piles of publishing companies. But an experienced slush pile reader can tell a really bad manuscript by the first few paragraphs and often will not read (and will not have to read) further. (After all, how far did I have to read to know that the ABC above was worthless?) It is the slush pile manuscripts that most often receive the printed rejection notes that tell you absolutely nothing about how close or far away your story was from acceptance.

But if you are able to get into pile number two by dint of having an agent or a friend of a friend—or even by taking a course in writing with a published author who takes an interest in your manuscripts—then you are most likely to receive a letter explaining *why* your manuscript has been turned down, if it is turned down.

Responding to rejection

Please do not be discouraged by one or two or three rejection letters. Everyone gets them. My Caldecott Honor Book was turned down by six publishers before winning acceptance. Madeleine L'Engle's Newbery winner, *A Wrinkle in Time,* was rejected by thirty publishing companies. Every published author can tell you similar tales.

After the first five rejection letters, reread the book again yourself. Ask yourself that difficult question: *are they right?* If your answer is an objective no, then send it on to five more. If you are being honest with yourself and you have a basis for your belief (having read many books in the genre), your manuscript will eventually be accepted. Why? Because somewhere out there is an editor who has as much taste as you have.

If you do receive a printed form rejection letter, it is useless to try to guess what it means. It could be that your manuscript is no good at all, that it is too similar to another book on the publisher's list, that the publisher does not publish that kind of book, or any number of reasons in between. But if the editor has taken time to scribble a few words on the printed form, you have every right to be encouraged. Editors do not arbitrarily take time to encourage authors they think are absolutely unsavable. If they have taken time to note something down on your manuscript, it is precisely because they wish to encourage you.

If you receive a typed rejection letter, it means that your manuscript was highly considered and you may try to read between the lines. "Not right for our list" is one of those phrases that can mean the editor is interested in the writer— but not in that book. However, more often it is a polite way of saying "no" and a lot easier on one's ego than "This is awful." It should not give you any false hope for the manuscript. Count it simply as a rejection. If the editor spells out just what he or she feels is wrong with the book, consider the criticisms carefully. And be sure to send *that* editor your next manuscript, citing the nice letter you received about your last book, its title, and the date of the letter.

Of course if the letter you receive is an acceptance letter, you have a whole new series of problems opening up before you. But they are all problems with a happy ending.

There is only one kind of acceptance letter you must be wary of, and that is the letter that says: "We want to publish your book, and it will only cost you $2000." No reputable publishing company charges you anything for the privilege of publishing your book. They pay you for that privilege. A company that charges for the service is called a "vanity publisher." It is a glorified printing company that preys on the vanities (and they are numerous) of would-be authors. The rule of thumb is—the publisher pays you, not you the publisher.

If you receive neither a rejection nor an acceptance letter in six weeks, write a nudging letter to the editor. By two months, you can send a strong letter. By three, make a phone call to the publishing company. By four, send a registered letter of inquiry, and if that brings no response, complain to the post office.

There is no reason why an editor should take more than six weeks for the reading of a simple manuscript, especially if it is only two to three pages long. But things do happen that slow down the reading sessions: an assistant gets married or gets sick; a manuscript gets misplaced or misfiled; an editor is interested but checking out the competition; it is sales conference time or vacation time or library convention time instead of manuscript-reading time.

These things do happen. But by three months you have every right to scream. However, do not mistake the amount of time taken for genuine interest in your manuscript. Sometimes it is true that a number of people are reading the book and that is why it is taking so long. Just as often, a number of people have been too busy to read the book, and that is why it has taken so long. Another rule of thumb: time does not equal interest—necessarily.

The business side

Wonder of wonders, your book has been accepted for publication. Not really that surprising, but still each sale is always a minor miracle. I celebrate each time with just as much joy as the first.

What can you expect now?

First, if you do not have an agent to do it for you, you will discuss the terms of your contract with your editor. A face-to-face meeting is best, but a telephone conference will do. If neither is possible, letter-to-letter will suffice.

The terms of the contract include how much money the author will receive, how soon the book will be printed, what happens if the book is sold to the movies or to a reprint house or to a foreign publisher. The contract will also spell out the responsibilities of both the author (no libel, no obscenities, no plagiarism, a clean copy of an acceptable manuscript) and the publisher (royalty statements at specified times, books kept in print as long as feasible, selling the book at a certain cost.) If you have no idea what a good contract should include, write to the Authors Guild (234 West 44th Street, New York, New York 10036) or the Society of Children's Book Writers (P.O. Box 296, Mar Vista Station, Los Angeles, California 90066) for advice. Or consult a lawyer. At the very least, have your editor explain each of the clauses and subclauses to you. Take special note of the "option" clause. This means that the publisher gets a first look at your next book. You can request that this be struck out, or that the words "next book on terms to be agreed upon," be inserted. This clause is both a good and bad one. It is good in that it indicates your publisher's desire and intent to publish more by you. It is bad in that it binds you to the publishers even if they treat you shabbily. In my contracts, option clauses are either limited or struck out altogether.

The words "advance" and "royalty" always seem to puzzle new authors, but there is nothing simpler. An advance is the publisher's way of telling you they expect the book to sell *at least* that much. For example, if you receive an advance of $1000 and 10% royalty, that means that when your book has sold enough copies to make up that original advance, the

publisher will start sending you more. It is a kind of loan
(but be sure the contract says a "non-returnable advance" so
that they do not ask for the kind-of-loan back) and a kind of
payment for your work. Further in the example, if your book
sells for $10, with your 10% royalty, you will receive 10%
of every book sold, or $1 per book. When 1000 copies of the
book have sold, you have $1000, or the exact amount of the
advance. You have earned the advance. Everything else, any
books sold now—as they say—is gravy. Twice a year the
publisher totals up the amount of books sold times your royalty percentage and makes an accounting to you. If you have
made up the advance, a check for the difference will be forth-
coming. (But check the addition yourself. I have twice caught
publishing companies in errors—against me. They are, after
all, only human!)

Revisions

Once a book has been accepted and a contract drawn up,
that is not the end of your responsibilities but a new beginning. You—and many other people—now have jobs to per-
form to turn your manuscript into a finished book.

The very first job may well be yours, for the editor may
feel the book needs to be revised. I have always welcomed re-
vising, though many people dread the manuscript's return.
But think of the word *revision;* it means looking again, en-
visioning anew, seeing with someone else's eyes. It can be an
exciting and very creative part of making the book. As
Phyllis A. Whitney says, "Good stories are not written, they
are rewritten."

Another job may be finding a new title. Some authors—I
am among them—have Title-itis. It is a disease of creating
a book's title before the actual book comes to mind. Other
authors are title-phobes and cannot come up with a name for

the book without the aid of an editor and the sales force. At least five times, I have had my original titles changed —and each time for the better. *Trust a City Kid* was first called *Roachy*; *Greyling* was known as *Silky* in manuscript; *Hobo Toad and the Motorcycle Gang* was plain *Hobo Toad*; I had originally called *Neptune Rising* the more elliptical and uninformative *Mer*; and I wanted to call this book on writing for children *There Would Be Unicorns*, a romantic and intriguing title for a fantasy novel, but it hardly describes the subject or substance. Titles are important. They catch the reader's ear the way a book jacket catches his eye. A good title can be an aid in selling a book.

Editing

Once a book has been accepted, revised, titled, and returned, it is ready for editing. That means that someone at the publishing house, often a copy editor whose main job in life that is, will check your story word for word for spelling mistakes, errors in punctuation, and any other small item that might spoil the story. It is up to the copy editor to be alert to any mistakes for he is the last checker on the manuscript before it goes to the printer.

At the printer, the book is set into *galleys*. These are long sheets of paper on which the text of your book is printed in a typeface picked out by either the editor or the designer. Several complete sets of the galleys are sent back to the publishing company to be proofread and checked for errors, and one of these sets will be sent to you.

It will be the first time you will see your book "in print." The feeling you have will be a combination of fright and flattery. Suddenly the book is *real*. You sent out a badly typed manuscript and were sent back Truth. It may be only moments or hours or it may be days before you are ready to sit down and edit Truth. But edit it you must. With a good steady eye and ruthless pen you must go over every last word. Be sure each and every word is exactly what you want because this is probably your last chance at the thing. After that, the book will be untouchable. But change or add or subtract at this point with infinite care. Changing what is in print is expensive—and by contract, you may be charged for making too many such changes.

If your book is a picture book or a book with pictures, the editor will talk to you about the illustrator chosen for the book. If you are lucky (or you insist), you will see sketches or a dummy or at least the final drawings before they are printed. Take time to look at them carefully with a copy of your text at hand. There are always artists who forget to read *your* book with care, and add fillips of their own that actually contradict the text: Where the text says the child placed a mittened hand on the sled, the picture shows the hand quite bare; where the story mentions a cat's straight whiskers, the illustrator has drawn curly ones. Every artist is a creator and you must tactfully point out where your creation and the artist's are at odds. The editor will point out discrepancies, too. But sometimes a busy editor misses something. After all, she is working with a number of books. A not-so-busy author must be alert to catch such mistakes— and *not be afraid to mention them.*

Author-editor relationships

It is an important point—this fear. Especially on a first book, an author is afraid to throw a spanner in the works. What if, you muse, I say the wrong thing and they take back their promise to publish my book?

First, by contract they cannot.

Second (and I admit it is difficult to see this when it is

your first book), it is more important to have the book published correctly than published hastily.

The best kind of relationship that an editor and an author can have is one based on mutual respect.

Unlike some authors I know, I do not believe that authors and editors are natural enemies. Rather, they are symbiotes. They need one another to exist.

It is easy to see why an editor needs the writer. But there are also three good reasons why a writer needs an editor (and not just because few authors have the money to publish their work in the manner to which they would like to become accustomed). First, an editor has a broad knowledge of the field, an historical perspective. Second, the editor also has a broad knowledge of the marketability of a piece. And third —and perhaps more immediately important to the author— the editor is a *second eye,* reading and reporting accurately and constructively his or her reactions to the book.

But it is far easier for an editor to find a good writer than for a writer to find a good editor. This fact of publishing explains why writers follow a good editor from publishing house to publishing house. I have done it myself.

What makes a good editor? My good editor may not be yours, but I have six criteria:

1. *Honesty.* The editor must tell me at all times what is right and wrong with my work, for we must both be ruthless with my writing.

2. *Responsive.* The editor must answer phone calls and letters from me when I am miles away and unable to cope with certain problems. In other words, the editor must not act as though I am an annoyance, an intrusion, but welcome our connection.

3. *Ombudsman.* The editor must be my personal representative to the publishing company, fighting my fights with

production and sales departments, school and library people, and the like.

4. *Vision.* The editor must see beyond my words to their meaning and, if necessary, help me pull out those meanings from my words.

5. *Ego-tending.* The editor must be aware of me as a person, too, and help with the care and feeding of my ego when I need it. (And be ready to kick me where it may do the most good, if I need that, too!)

6. *Respect.* The editor must respect me as a writer—my integrity, my vision, my talent. In turn, I must respect the editor, his or her knowledge and competence. And we both must respect the language, its beauty, its treachery, its power to change lives.

The process of book making

After the galleys have gone back to the editor, the entire publishing company gears up. The printer makes corrections and runs off page proofs. These are corrected and any last minute changes are made. Then back to the printer where the final complex machinery is set to work. The presses roll out huge sheets of paper on which sixteen of your book's pages are printed at once on a single sheet of paper.

These *proofs* are once again read and checked. If the book is a picture book, these are color proofs and are gone over at the publishing house by editor and production staff with great care. The illustrator goes over them, too.

Then the editor gives the printer the O.K., the printer makes the final corrections, and then makes his final run. Enough of the large sheets are printed to make (for an ordinary children's book) 7500–10,000 copies.

The pages, packed in a plain brown wrapper, are shipped to the bindery.

Now while the printer is running off the large sheets on which the entire book is printed, the editor and designer back in the publishing house are busy with other details. For example, they are deciding upon a binding for the book. There are many color choices and grades of cloth or other materials to choose from.

When the sheets arrive at the bindery, they are fitted onto a huge machine that folds and cuts them on three sides and stitches them on the fourth. They are then put into the binding case, on go the jackets—and the first copies are then shipped to the editor who sends one off to you.

This is, of course, a highly simplified version of what is happening to your manuscript while you wait at home biting your nails or, hopefully, working on your next book.

When the process is complete, the editor will send you ten free copies of *your* book which you will no doubt show off and give away until you realize that the next copies you get from the publisher you will have to pay for. At a 40% discount, of course, but you have to pay nonetheless.

Still, you are published. Things are now in the hands of the sales force, the promotion department, the schools and libraries, the bookstores, the reviewers, and ultimately, the young readers. A process that once-upon-a-time took a single person with a goosequill pen writing a book, making handbound copies, and distributing them to his friends is no longer so simple. With the over two thousand new children's books that are produced yearly, approximately six months and hundreds of people are involved in each production. That does not even begin to count the author's original time.

The rewards

Is it worth it?

It is worth it the first time you open your mail and find your finished book there. It may look different from what you had originally envisioned. After all, a number of creative minds have been at work on it as well as your own—an illustrator, an editor, a designer. But it is yours.

It is worth it when it is first reviewed. Whether that review is good or bad, the book (*your* book) has been noticed. The state of reviewing children's books publicly in this country has had a short and ignoble tradition. Except for *The Horn Book, The New York Times, Publishers Weekly,* and *School Library Journal,* there are no major mass media that review books for young readers regularly. Many magazines and newspapers review children's books at Christmas or even twice a year. The books do get reviews in trade publications and library journals, and each school system has a way of looking over all the new books during the year. Your editor will probably send you a selection of these reviews.

It is worth it the first time you see your book in a library or bookstore. Of course, you are more likely to see it in a library, since 70% of children's book sales are to libraries.

It is worth it the first time you receive a royalty statement. Few children's books ever become best sellers in the way some adult novels do. Except for *Jonathan Livingston Seagull* (Richard Bach), *Watership Down* (Richard Adams), *A Light in the Attic* (Shel Silverstein), *Masquerade* (Kit Williams) and *The Lord of the Rings* (Tolkien), there has been no children's book on the best-seller list in several years. But then, relatively few adult books make the best-seller lists, either. Fortunately, because such a large percentage of children's books sell to libraries, even those that are not best sellers have a life of five to ten years, and at the very best, go on "forever."

It is worth it the first time your book is up for one of the major awards in the children's book field: the Caldecott Medal for "the most distinguished picture book"; the Newbery Medal for "the most distinguished contribution to children's literature"; The American Book Award; the William Allen White Award; the Society of Children's Book Writers' "Golden Kite Award"; and a number of others.

But the time it is most worth it is when you receive your first letter from a child reader in hard-to-read script or belabored print.

Dear Miss Jane Yolen,

I really loved the humorous book called *The Witch Who Wasn't*. Would you please write to Arnold Roth and tell him the pictures were marvelous? Would you please write to the Macmillan publishers and tell them that they picked a wonderful book to publish?

Love,
Susan Lawler

Are you sure it is worth it? Because of all the Susan Lawlers, you bet it is.

*There never were in the world two opinions
alike, no more than two hairs or two grains;
the most universal quality is diversity.*
                              —Michel de Montaigne

Afterword

A Child's Garden
of Voices

HERE IS an idiosyncratic reading list for anyone interested in
writing or reading about children's books. To paraphrase the
Bible, there is a time for writing and a time for reading. If
it is your time for reading, one or more of the following are
definite musts.

Books, Children, and Men, by Paul Hazard (Horn Book).
Probably the best single book in print today about *books, children,* and *men.* If you read no other work about juvenile literature, read this poetic treatise, this joyous hymn to children's books. Available in both hardcover and paperback.

Only Connect, edited by Egoff, Stubbs, and Ashley (Oxford
University Press). Vintage essays on children's literature,
including one I have quoted frequently here: "On Three Ways

of Writing for Children," by C. S. Lewis. Worth buying, if only for that essay.

The Green and Burning Tree, by Eleanor Cameron (Atlantic-Little Brown). One of the most stimulating books on books I have ever read. Ms. Cameron is a fantasy writer herself, and this is a brilliant book on the writing and reading of fantasy.

Down the Rabbit Hole, by Selma G. Lanes (Atheneum). A witty and perceptive group of essays on a variety of children's literature subjects. Even when you disagree with Mrs. Lanes, you will be impressed with her knowledge. Subjects include Seuss, Sendak, Potter, series books, "relevant" books, and the like.

Children and Books, by May Hill Arbuthnot (Scott Foresman). *The* tome for anyone interested in a general overall view of children's books from the beginning. It is the mainstay of children's literature courses (called Kiddy Lit by unperceptive students). Not a book to read in one sitting, but an outstanding reference volume for your shelf.

A Critical History of Children's Literature, by Meigs, Eaton, Nesbit, and Viguers (Macmillan). Another tome to add to your shelf, by four experts in the field of children's literature. More readable and less specific than the Arbuthnot. The two together cover—with love—everything in the field but "how to write."

Writing Juvenile Fiction, by Phyllis A. Whitney (The Writer, Inc.). A fast-paced and breezy book of advice from a well-known practitioner of the fast-paced and breezy kind of book for adults and teen-agers. Some excellent suggestions if not exactly heavy on insights into literature.

From Childhood to Childhood, by Jean Karl (John Day). Excellent advice and insights into children's books, by one of the top editors in the business. Written with facility and charm.

Matters of Fact, by Margery Fisher (Crowell) deals with aspects of nonfiction for children. An Englishwoman, the author's examples are more from British than American books, but she addresses herself to the problems of selecting and judging nonfiction books with depth and much critical insight.

Written for Children, by John Rowe Townsend (Lothrop). Subtitled "An Outline of English Children's Literature," this is a literate but dense account of literature for children from 15th century England to the present day.

The Children's Picture Book: How To Write It, How To Sell It, by Ellen E. Roberts (Writer's Digest), a thorough, workmanlike how-to book that details everything from getting ideas to the proper clauses in a contract. Specific and very helpful.

The Cool Web: The Pattern of Children's Reading, by Margaret Meek, et. al. (Atheneum), a collection of essays by distinguished authors and critics and linked by the editors' commentaries. Strong, intelligent reading.

Fairy Tales and After: From Snow White to E.B. White, by Roger Sale (Harvard University Press). Idiosyncratic readings in children's literature by an English professor. Often insightful, occasionally wrong-headed, and full of a quirky charm.

Books: From Writer to Reader, by Howard Greenfeld (Crown), warm, witty, well written, with undeniably the best section on the process a book goes through after it leaves the author's typewriter that I have ever read. Highly recommended.

Writing for Young Children, by Claudia Lewis (Penguin), considered a classic in the genre, strong, well-thought-out advice from a teacher who helped run the famous Bank Street Writers workshop for years.

Writing Mysteries for Young People, by Joan Lowery Nixon (The Writer, Inc.) is good professional advice from someone who knows what she is talking about. Nixon is a past winner of the Mystery Writers of America award for best juvenile mystery book and a member of the Mystery Writers of America.

Children's Literature: An Issues Approach, by Masha Kabakow Rudman (Heath). An insightful look at literature from the educator's point of view. Dr. Rudman tackles children's books that touch on or deal with such issues as Death, Old Age, War, Divorce, Sex, etc. But she never denies the importance of literature, of style, of the story. Must reading.

Children and Literature: Views and Reviews, by Virginia Haviland (Scott, Foresman). A collection of essays from C. S. Lewis's "On Three Ways of Writing for Children," to pieces on international children's book publishing. The many articles, essays, and book selections have been chosen with loving care and a great deal of wisdom by the editor, who is head of the Library of Congress children's book section. A necessary addition to any library.

Index